# Developing Good Health

**Third Edition**

abeka®
Pensacola, FL 32523-9100
an affiliate of PENSACOLA CHRISTIAN COLLEGE®

# Elementary Science & Health Series

## Science

K5  *God's World K5*

Grade 1  *Discovering God's World*

2  *Enjoying God's World*

3  *Exploring God's World*

4  *Understanding God's World*

5  *Investigating God's World*

6  *Observing God's World*

(Support materials and Grades 7–12 materials also available.)

## Health

- *Health, Safety, and Manners 1*
- *Health, Safety, and Manners 2*
- *Health, Safety, and Manners 3*
- **Developing Good Health**
- *Enjoying Good Health*
- *Choosing Good Health*

*abeka*®

## *Developing Good Health*

Third Edition

**Staff Credits**

*Author:* Delores Shimmin
*Edition Editor:* Marion Hedquist
*Designer:* T. J. Nikkel
*Illustrators:* Paul DeLuna, Stan Shimmin, Jonathan Taylor, Matthew Sample II,
        Bill Bailey, Scott Lyle, Chris Martinez

Cataloging Data
Shimmin, Delores.
    Developing good health / Delores Shimmin. —3rd ed.
    v, 110 p. : col. ill. ; 26 cm. — (Abeka Book science and
    health series)
    Includes index.
    1. Health education (Elementary)  II. Abeka Book, Inc.
Library of Congress:  RA440 .S25 D48  2008
Dewey System:  372.3

# Contents

# Unit ② Personal Hygiene

# Unit 3 Right Relationships

## Pronunciation Key

| Symbol • Example | | Symbol • Example | |
|---|---|---|---|
| ā | āte | ŏ | nŏt |
| â | dâre | oi | boil |
| ă | făt | o͞o | fo͞od |
| ä | fäther | o͝o | bo͝ok |
| ə | ago (ə·gō′) | ou | out |
| ē | ēven | th | thin |
| ĕ | ĕgg | t̶h̶ | t̶h̶ere |
| ẽ (ər) | pondẽr | t̯ṷ | pict̯ṷre |
| ī | īce | ū | ūnit |
| ĭ | ĭt | û | hûrt |
| ō | ōver | ŭ | ŭp |
| ô | côrd, taught, saw | zh | measure |

# chapter 1

# Your Body's Framework

## Fearfully and wonderfully made

How tall are you?  How much do you weigh?  When you are outside during physical education class, look at the various members of your class.  You are all about the same age, but you are not all the same height or weight.  Some are much taller than others, and some can run faster than others.  You can see many differences in physical appearance.

When God planned you before you were born, He designed the color of your eyes, skin, and hair, the shape of your nose, your height, and your other physical features.  He also planned when you would be born, what parents you would have, and whether you would be a boy or a girl.

You cannot change the color of your eyes, nor can you make your body grow any taller or any shorter than God created you to be.  Have you ever thanked God for making you just as He did?  The Bible says, "I will praise thee; for I am fearfully and wonderfully made" (Psa. 139:14).

Some things about your body you cannot change, because God created you to be that way—He created you for a special purpose.  Some things about you can be changed, however, and they may need changing.  Look at yourself in a mirror.  Do you look clean and neat?  Is your hairstyle becoming?  Do you look pleasant?  God designed the shape of your mouth, but only you can make it smile!  As you learn more about your body and how to keep it healthy, try to determine what things you may need to change and what things you cannot change.

## Support for your body

As you grow taller, the bones in your body grow larger. Your *206 bones* make a strong *framework for your body.* This bony framework, called your **skeleton,** gives your body its shape and helps to hold it up. The skeleton also protects important organs in your body.

In order for your skeleton to support your body, your bones must be joined together. Tough fibers or cords called **ligaments** hold the bones together. The places where the bones come together are called **joints.** Many joints in your body are movable. There are three main kinds of freely movable joints in the

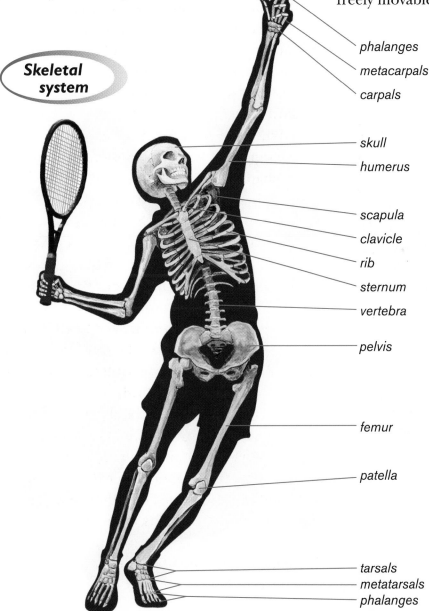

Skeletal system

phalanges
metacarpals
carpals

skull
humerus

scapula
clavicle
rib
sternum
vertebra

pelvis

femur

patella

tarsals
metatarsals
phalanges

skeleton—the hinge joint, the ball-and-socket joint, and the pivot joint. Your knees, elbows, and fingers are called **hinge joints** because they swing back and forth like a hinge on a door. **Ball-and-socket joints,** such as the shoulders and hips, allow you to move your arms and legs in many directions. A **pivot joint** lets you move your head from side to side. Your elbow has a hinge joint and a pivot joint. Hold your arm out straight with the palm of your hand down. Now turn the palm of your hand up. The pivot joint lets you turn a doorknob or use a screwdriver.

## Quick Checkup

1. How many bones make up the framework for your body?
2. What is the framework for your body called?
3. What are the tough fibers or cords that hold the bones together?
4. What are the places where bones come together called?
5. Name the three kinds of joints in your body.

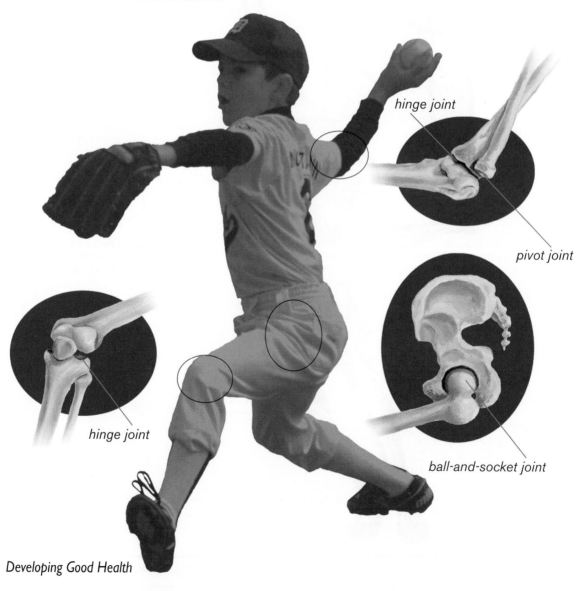

hinge joint

pivot joint

hinge joint

ball-and-socket joint

I am tough, solid tissue with a whitish color like a translucent milk glass. Unlike other living tissue, I do not have any blood vessels in me. Does it puzzle you how I can get my food and energy when I have no blood vessels to bring them? The Creator God attached me firmly to the end of each bone in your body. You can feel me at the end of your nose. Wherever one bone touches another bone, I am there. Because the Lord attached me to your bones, I can get food and energy from the blood in them.

If the Son of God had not put me between your bones, there would be a terrible vibration and grinding every time you bent one of your joints. The ends of your bones would rub against each other, and soon the joints would become

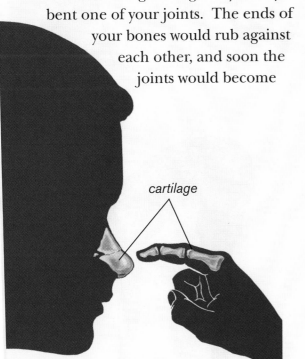

cartilage

inflamed (red and swollen) and extremely painful.

I am in the hinge in your elbow, finger, and knee and in the ball-and-socket in your shoulder and hip. I can be found any place you can bend. All hinges need lubrication (oil) to work smoothly, so the intelligent Master Designer put a special factory in each joint. These factories produce a unique liquid called *synovial fluid*. They are engineered to constantly coat all joints with this slippery fluid. This is the reason your joints move smoothly, quietly, and painlessly.

I seldom become diseased, because I am well protected by your body's self-defense system. I do get torn though, through abuse. If I am pulled away from the end of one of your bones, I usually will not reattach. Then the doctor may have to remove me and replace me with a plastic or steel joint. If you take care of me, I will last you for seventy years or more.

I am only one kind of cartilage that you have in your body. Feel how flexible your ear is. Its framework is elastic cartilage. Another kind of cartilage which is very tough acts as a shock absorber between the bones of your spinal column (backbone).

—Bob Devine

# Designer bones

Your bones were designed in a wide variety of shapes—some long, some short, some round, and some flat. Each bone is the right shape for its particular job. Your **spinal column,** or backbone, is your body's main support. Without it you could not sit or stand. The adult spinal column is made up of thirty-three small bones called **vertebrae** [vûr′tə·brā′], which are joined together by slightly movable joints so that you can bend and twist your spine. Each bone in the spinal column is called a **vertebra** [vûr′tə·brə]. The design of your spine makes it possible for you to bend over, and it also makes it necessary for

you to practice keeping your backbone straight when you sit, stand, or walk.

The spinal column has another important function besides helping you to sit and stand. It forms a hollow tube of bone that protects your delicate spinal cord. This important cord, which enables your body to feel and to move, could be damaged by poor posture.

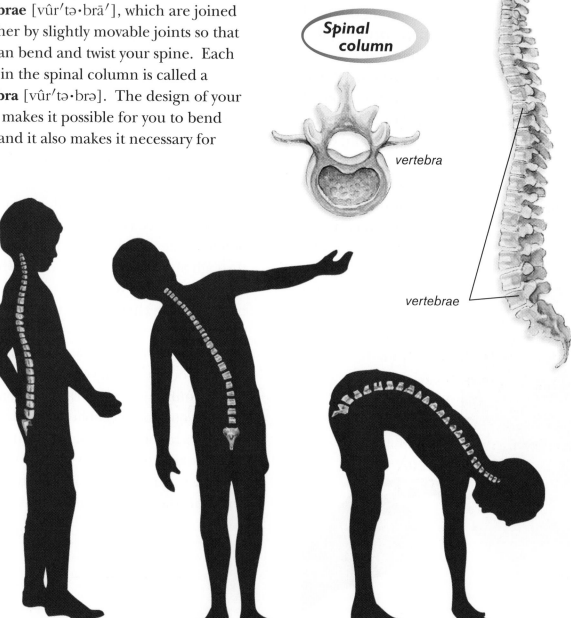

*Spinal column*

*vertebra*

*vertebrae*

Your ribs are long, thin bones which form a **rib cage** to protect your heart and lungs. Each pair of ribs is attached to a separate vertebra. All of the ribs, except the two lowest ones on each side, are attached in the front to the **sternum,** or breastbone.

The **clavicle** [klăv′ĭ·kəl], or collarbone, is a long, slender bone that connects the sternum to the **scapula** [skăp′yə·lə], or shoulder blade. You have two clavicles that hold your arms in the proper position at the sides of your body. When a clavicle is broken, the shoulder drops down toward the chest.

Another part of the skeleton that protects you is your **skull**— twenty-two bones which shield your brain, ears, and eyes from injuries. The skull bones are held together by immovable joints. The eight flat bones that enclose your brain form the **cranium** [krā′nē·əm]. The skull also forms the shape of your face. The **facial bones,** except the lower jawbone, attach to the two upper jawbones. Your lower jawbone, which moves when you open and close your mouth, is the only facial bone that moves.

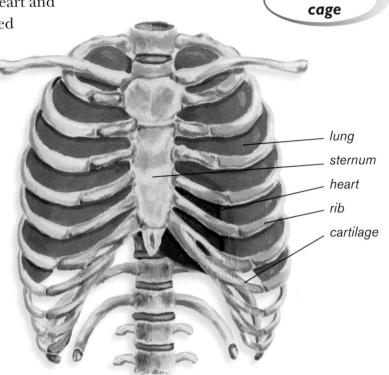

Rib cage

lung
sternum
heart
rib
cartilage

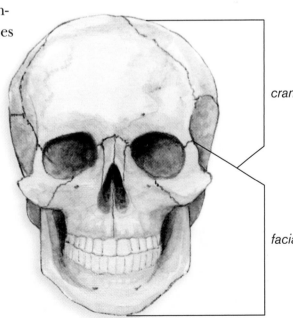

cranium

facial bones

You have twenty-seven bones in each hand. Eight of these bones are **carpals** [kär′pəlz], or wrist bones. Five long hand bones, called **metacarpals,** are found in the palm of your hand; these bones connect the carpals to your fingers. Each of your fingers has three slender bones called **phalanges** [fə·lăn′jēz]; your thumbs have only two. Without your phalanges it would be difficult to grasp, hold onto, pick up, or pull something. Try tying your shoes, pitching a ball, or writing without using your phalanges. The toe bones, which are also called phalanges, are shorter and broader than the phalanges in your fingers, because your toes help you keep your body balanced when you stand or walk.

## Quick Checkup

1. How many bones make up the adult spinal column?

2. What bones protect your heart and lungs?

3. Give another name for each bone.
   a. breastbone    c. shoulder blade
   b. collarbone    d. wrist bones

4. What do we call the top part of your skull (made up of eight bones)?

5. Name the five long bones in your palm.

6. What are your heel and ankle bones called?

7. Name the bones that make up the fingers and toes.

8. What do we call the bones of your foot between the tarsals and phalanges?

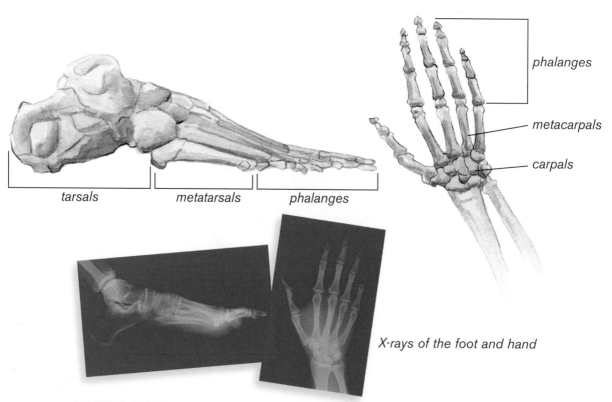

tarsals          metatarsals          phalanges

phalanges

metacarpals

carpals

X-rays of the foot and hand

Study the picture of the human skeleton on page 3 and then label the bones below. Can you pronounce the scientific name for each of these bones?

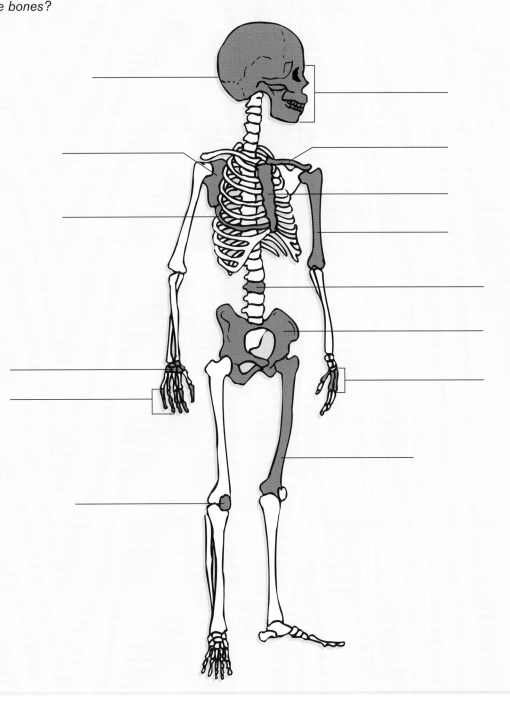

# Nutrients Your Body Needs
*(You will refer to this chart throughout the book.)*

| Nutrient | Good Sources | Function |
|---|---|---|
| **Protein** | Lean meats, fish, poultry, eggs, milk, buttermilk, powdered milk, yogurt, cheese, soybeans, yeast, wheat germ, legumes <br> *You need milk and other protein food every day.* | Enables your body to grow <br> Builds muscles <br> Fights infection <br> Repairs your body <br> Helps your body function properly |
| **Carbohydrates** | Fruits, vegetables, whole-grain breads and cereals, brown rice, seeds, nuts, dried beans and peas, honey <br> *The more active you are, the more you need.* | Give energy for physical activity <br> Help heat your body <br> Allow your body to use protein for growth and repair <br> Help your body use fats |
| **Fats** | Cooking oil, butter, margarine, mayonnaise, cheese, whole milk, egg yolk, nuts, peanut butter, seeds, wheat germ <br> *You need only a small amount every day.* | Carry vitamins A, D, E, and K to all parts of your body <br> Give an extra supply of energy <br> Help keep your body warm <br> Help keep your skin from becoming dry and flaky <br> Keep you from feeling hungry |
| **Fiber** | Whole-grain breads and cereals, bran, raw fruits and vegetables, fruits with seeds (figs, berries), nuts <br> *You need some every day.* | Helps eliminate waste materials |
| **Liquids** | Milk, fruit juice, vegetable juice, water <br> *You need about 6 glasses every day.* | Help control body temperature <br> Carry nutrients throughout your body <br> Help digest food <br> Help change food into energy <br> Help to produce blood, saliva, and digestive juices <br> Carry wastes from your body |

*Minerals*

| Nutrient | Good Sources | Function |
|---|---|---|
| **Calcium** | Milk, buttermilk, yogurt, frozen yogurt, cheddar cheese, canned salmon and sardines (with bones), shellfish, dark green leafy vegetables (except spinach, chard, and beet greens), broccoli, soybeans, dried dates and figs, barley <br> *You need milk at every meal.* | Builds strong bones and teeth <br> Helps broken bones to mend <br> Prevents tooth decay <br> Regulates muscle contractions <br> Helps you relax |
| **Iodine** | Seafood, iodized salt | Helps your thyroid gland function properly |
| **Iron** | Liver, lean meat, shellfish, dark green leafy vegetables, egg yolk, soybeans, dried peas and beans, dried fruits, wheat germ, dark molasses, whole-grain breads and cereals | Keeps your blood healthy <br> Helps your body use oxygen <br> Prevents fatigue |
| **Magnesium** | Whole grains, soybeans, dried peas and beans, nuts, dark green leafy vegetables, potatoes, fruits, yeast, molasses <br> *You need extra whenever you are involved in strenuous or long-endurance activities.* | Helps change food into energy <br> Helps your body absorb calcium <br> Helps your circulatory system work properly <br> Regulates muscle contractions <br> Helps you relax |

| Nutrient | Good Sources | Function |
|---|---|---|
| **Phosphorus** | Milk, cheese, meat, fish, poultry, eggs, whole-grain breads and cereals, legumes, nuts | Builds strong bones and teeth<br>Helps regulate many body functions<br>Helps store and release energy |
| **Potassium** | Fruits, vegetables, soybeans, mushrooms, wheat germ, whole-grain breads and cereals, nuts, yeast, lean meats<br>*Eat more fruits and vegetables and fewer salty foods.* | Keeps your heartbeat regular<br>Helps your nervous system work properly<br>Helps you think clearly |
| **Zinc** | Shellfish, lean meat, poultry, eggs, whole grains, nuts | Helps repair your body<br>Heals wounds<br>Helps your immune system |

*Vitamins*

| Nutrient | Good Sources | Function |
|---|---|---|
| **Vitamin A** | Egg yolk, milk, fish-liver oils, liver, butter, enriched margarine, dark green vegetables, deep yellow fruits and vegetables<br>*You need to eat at least one dark green vegetable, one deep yellow vegetable, or one deep yellow fruit at two different meals each day.* | Helps keep your skin healthy and smooth<br>Helps you see well<br>Helps the development of bones and tooth enamel<br>Helps protect against colds and infections |
| **B vitamins** | Liver, yeast, wheat germ, brown rice, milk, meat, whole-grain breads and cereals, nuts, most vegetables<br>*You need some every day.* | Help your body use protein to build new tissue<br>Help change food into energy<br>Help the digestion of your food<br>Help your body grow at a normal rate<br>Help keep your blood healthy<br>Help keep your gums healthy and prevent tooth decay<br>Help keep the skin around your eyes and mouth smooth and healthy<br>Help your heart and nervous system work properly |
| **Vitamin C** | Citrus fruits, berries, papayas, cantaloupes, tomatoes, broccoli, raw cabbage, Brussels sprouts, green peppers<br>*You need some every day.* | Helps your body resist and fight infection<br>Helps heal cuts, scrapes, burns, and broken bones<br>Helps keep your gums healthy<br>Develops strong bones and teeth<br>Helps prevent allergies<br>Helps form the material that holds the body cells together<br>Helps prevent fatigue |
| **Vitamin D** | Milk fortified with vitamin D, liver, fish-liver oils, sardines, salmon, tuna, egg yolk | Helps your body use minerals from other foods to build strong bones and teeth<br>Helps prevent tooth decay |
| **Vitamin E** | Vegetable oils, wheat germ, whole-grain breads and cereals, egg yolk, liver, bean sprouts, cabbage, yeast, dark green leafy vegetables<br>*The more fats and oils you eat, the more vitamin E you need.* | Keeps nutrients from being destroyed in your body by oxygen<br>Helps your body use vitamin A<br>Increases the amount of vitamin A that can be stored in your liver<br>Helps change food into energy<br>Helps keep your heart and skeletal muscles healthy<br>Helps burns heal faster |
| **Vitamin K** | Yogurt, alfalfa sprouts, dark green leafy vegetables, cabbage, cauliflower, egg yolk, liver, soybean oil | Helps your blood clot properly |

# Building materials for strong bones

Your bones grow as your body grows. All bones are living tissue; thus they need good food to increase in size and strength. Bones are hard because of the large amount of minerals they contain. Your blood carries these minerals to your bones to make them strong. *Milk is especially important for building strong bones* because it contains **calcium** and **phosphorus,** important minerals that your bones need. Milk that is fortified with **vitamin D** helps the body to absorb calcium. Sunshine helps your skin to manufacture vitamin D in your body. Refer to the chart on pages 10 and 11 to find other good sources of calcium and vitamin D.

Good food helps build *strong* bones; good posture and exercise help build strong, *straight* bones. When your body is growing rapidly, you may sometimes feel awkward and clumsy because your strength and coordination have not caught up with your growth. Exercise aids bone growth and helps you to develop both strength and coordination. Any activity that makes you stronger and more flexible will help you to overcome that awkward feeling and make you more comfortable and sure of yourself.

Since your bones make it possible for you to hold your body correctly, correct posture is needed for the proper growth and development of your bones. Poor posture can force the bones to grow improperly, causing round shoulders, a flattened chest, or the wrong kind of curves in the spinal column.

**Healthful Hints** for building strong, straight bones

Eat the right kinds of food and drink plenty of milk.

Spend time in the sunshine.

Get plenty of exercise and practice good posture.

# Posture—as others see you

What do others see when they look at you? Do you appear confident? Happy? Full of energy? Probably the first thing others see is your **posture,** or *the way you hold your body when you sit, stand, or move about.* If you hold your body in the proper sitting and standing positions when you are young, the bones and muscles will grow properly and correct posture will become a **habit**—*something you do without thinking about it.*

When your posture is good, the parts of your body are in position to do the work God designed them to do. Good posture allows the lungs to expand and fill with air. It helps the blood to circulate freely through the body, and it aids in the digestion of food. When your posture is good, the weight of your body is supported as it should be, and you can sit, stand, or walk around without getting tired too soon. Because your bones and good posture work together, it is especially important to have good posture when you are growing.

If you let your body slouch or slump, your lungs, stomach, and other important organs become crowded, and your blood does not circulate well through your body. A lack of oxygen and poor circulation caused by poor posture make your body work harder than it should. Foot problems, back trouble, and headaches may also be caused by poor posture. Only when correct posture habits are used do the parts of the body work together in proper balance and comfort.

## Sitting properly

Because you spend more time sitting each day than you do standing or walking, your sitting posture is very important! When you are working at a table or desk, you will not get tired as easily if you sit on a straight, hard chair. The chair—instead of your muscles—can do much of the work of keeping your body straight. Sit back on your chair so that your hips touch the back of it. Sit tall with your shoulders pulled back and your back straight. Keep your abdomen in, and let your feet rest on the floor with your toes pointed forward. You should not cross your knees while you are sitting because that causes poor blood circulation. It also throws your body out of balance, causing poor posture. If you have to sit for a long time, it may be relaxing to cross your ankles for a few minutes, but you should return to the correct sitting posture.

If possible, you should occasionally stand up and stretch. This improves your circulation and helps keep you alert.

When you lean forward to get closer to your work, you should not let your shoulders and back slump. Bend from your hips so that your back stays straight. Whenever you find yourself sliding too far down into your seat or bending too far forward, you need to straighten up. Poor posture is lazy posture—it gives you a dull, tired feeling that keeps your body and mind from being alert and active. Good posture makes you look better, feel better, and have more energy.

Sitting improperly in a lounge chair can strain your neck and shoulders and cause poor posture. When you sit in a lounge chair, you may want to rest your legs and feet on an ottoman or footstool to help you relax. This also helps your circulation. If you are sitting correctly, your chest will expand easily.

Good posture does not mean stiff, rigid posture. If you are sitting properly, there should be no strain on any part of your body. You should look and feel comfortable.

## Quick Checkup

1. Name three things you should do to build strong, straight bones.

2. What vitamin is milk fortified with?

3. What do we call the way you hold your body?

4. What is a habit?

**EXERCISE 4 FITNESS**   **Shoulder Twist**

To help relax your muscles that are tired from sitting for a long time, stand with your feet apart and your hands on your hips. Hold your head high and turn your shoulders as far as you can to the left. Now turn them as far as you can to the right. Do this five to ten times.

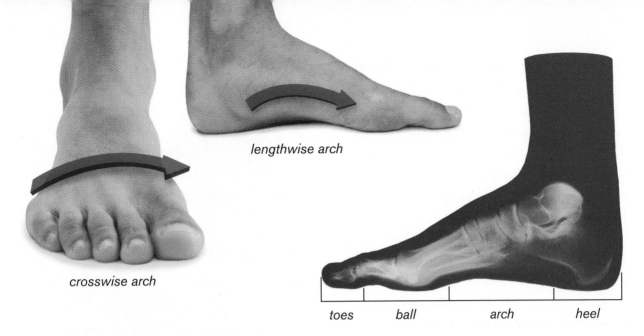

lengthwise arch

crosswise arch

toes     ball     arch     heel

## Standing correctly

*One fourth of all the bones in your body are in your feet.* Strong foot bones help you to have good standing posture. The long bones of your feet, or **metatarsals,** are arched so that they can support your body. If the arches of the feet lose their proper shape, the feet become flat, and walking or standing for a long time causes pain. Flat feet can be caused by wearing shoes that do not fit well, by walking with the toes pointed outward instead of straight ahead, or by not getting enough exercise and nourishing food to build strong bones and muscles.

When you are standing correctly, you are standing tall. Pretend that you are trying to touch the ceiling with the top of your head. Your feet should be two or three inches apart with your toes pointed straight ahead. Turning your toes inward or outward weakens your ankles. Your weight should be on the balls of your feet instead of on your heels or toes. Your back and shoulders should be held the same way they are when you are sitting correctly. Pull your abdomen in and your chest up. Let your arms relax at your sides.

Tickle Your **FUNNY** Bone

Question: What animal hates cold feet the most?
Answer: A mother kangaroo.

Question: What kind of cat has no feet?
Answer: A catfish.

Between the ages of ten and twelve, there is usually a noticeable increase in a child's height and weight. Girls usually begin this stage of growth before boys do. Sometimes boys and girls who suddenly become taller slouch or slump in order to hide their height. When they do this, however, their poor posture makes them more noticeable. How much better it is to stand tall and be thankful for the way God has made you!

To help get correct standing posture, stand with your heels about an inch from the wall. Your feet should be two or three inches apart, and your head, shoulders, and hips should touch the wall. To get your shoulders in the proper position, roll them up, back, and down. Remember—correct posture is not rigid posture. Your knees and shoulders should not be stiff; you should be able to move them freely.

Nice Posture!

## Walking with ease

If you stand correctly, you can walk correctly. Your legs should be close together as you lift each foot and move it forward. Put your heel down; then shift your weight first to the ball of your foot and then to the toes. Keep your toes pointed straight ahead so that the weight of your body will be divided evenly over the ball of the foot and all the toes. You should swing your legs forward from the hip joint for free and easy movement. Do not place one foot directly in front of the other, as this causes poor balance. Your body should be relaxed with your arms swinging freely at your sides as you walk. Is your back straight? Your head high? Your shoulders back? Your abdomen in? Do not slide or shuffle your feet along, but walk as if you were full of energy. This will help you to feel more confident.

To check your posture, walk in front of a full-length mirror. Is your body straight and tall? Do you look comfortable? Now look at the expression on your face. If you have a bored or sour expression on your face, other people may not like to be around you. If you smile and look friendly, the pleasant expression on your face will cause other people to want to be with you. Good posture and a happy smile work together to give you a pleasant appearance.

You will not be able to walk correctly in shoes that are the wrong size. When you are buying new shoes, be sure to try on both shoes. There should be plenty of room for your toes. Shoes that fit properly give support to your arches, and they are broad enough so that your foot rests flat on the sole when all of your weight is on one foot. Wearing shoes that are too narrow cramps the crosswise arch and keeps it from doing its work. Shoes that do not fit can change the shape of the feet, making them work harder to support the weight of the body. Poorly fitted shoes can also disfigure the feet. Low-heeled or flat shoes with broad toes give girls better balance and a more graceful walk than high-heeled shoes.

Your socks should also fit well; be sure they are not too small. Tight clothing or shoes may cause poor posture because they do not allow your bones to grow correctly. Shoes that are too large may cause blisters.

If you carry heavy loads of books, your body will have better balance if you carry some in both arms or carry them in a backpack. If you do carry them all in one arm or carry a heavy shoulder bag or musical instrument, change them occasionally from side to side.

## Bending carefully

Much of your work and play involves bending. Poor posture can make you tire easily, or it can hurt your back. Do you help your mother vacuum the floor? Do not let your body slump forward. Lean forward with your body in a straight line from your head to the heel of your back foot. Then you can use your arm and leg muscles to push.

If you are playing a board game on the floor, you should keep your back straight whenever you bend over. Kneel close to the game and bend forward at your hip joints.

Remember to use good posture when you work in the yard or garden. What other work might you bend over to do? Remember to bend forward at your hip joints and keep your back straight.

*correct*                    *incorrect*

## Lifting correctly

If you lift heavy objects with your back muscles instead of your strong leg and arm muscles, you can strain or hurt the muscles in your lower back. *Whenever you lift an object, instead of bending over from your waist, keep your back straight and bend your knees.* Get a good grip on the object before you start to lift it. As you lift, be sure that the object is close to your body and that your back is straight.

The amount of rest you get also affects your posture. Tired muscles cannot hold your body straight. Weak muscles allow your shoulders to sag forward and your whole body to slump. Your body needs good food to build muscles; it needs exercise to build strong muscles. Your bones will grow straight if your muscles are strong enough to hold your body up.

Although many things affect your posture, good or poor posture is usually a habit. You must *want* to have good posture. Work at improving your posture until it becomes a habit to sit tall, stand tall, and walk tall. You will look better, your mind will be more alert, and you will have a feeling of being able to do your best at work and play.

**Tug of War**

Divide into two teams and have each team pull at one end of a rope. Mark the center line on the ground. The team that pulls the opposite team across the center line first is the winner. Your feet should be apart, and your back straight. Bend your knees so that you can push with your front foot while you pull with your arms. This lets your arm and leg muscles do all the work.

If you have a large group, use two ropes of the same length and tie them together in the middle. Make a large + on the ground to mark

the center lines. Count off in ones, twos, threes, and fours and have each number form a line along one part of the center lines. At the starting signal, each team pulls. The first team to pull its opposite team across any part of the center line is the winner.

Remember to stand with your feet apart, your back straight, and your knees bent so that you can push with your front foot while you pull with your arms. Ready? TUG!

**Healthful Habits** for good posture

Head up.
Shoulders back.
Back straight.
Abdomen in.
Toes forward.

Your Body's Framework **19**

# Chapter Checkup

A. Study the skeletal system diagram on page 3.

B. Identify each bone.
   1. a leg bone
   2. a wrist bone
   3. the breastbone
   4. an arm bone
   5. the collarbone
   6. a long bone of the foot
   7. the flat bones of the skull
   8. one bone of the spinal column
   9. an ankle bone
   10. the finger or toe bones
   11. a long bone of the hand
   12. a shoulder blade

C. Define each term.
   1. habit
   2. joint
   3. ligament
   4. posture
   5. rib cage
   6. skeleton

D. Answer each question.
   1. What is another name for your backbone?
   2. Which type of joint lets the head move from side to side?
   3. Which type of joint allows the arm and leg to move in many directions?
   4. Which type of joint allows the knee to move back and forth?
   5. Why is good posture important?

# The Muscle Builder

# chapter 2

## Six hundred workers

Your skeleton is the framework for your body, but your muscles share the work of supporting your weight and holding you up. *All of your movements are made by muscles.* God designed you with *over 600 muscles,* which are different shapes and sizes according to the work they do. Without muscles, you could not eat, your heart would not beat, you could not breathe, and you could not move.

## Your skeletal muscles

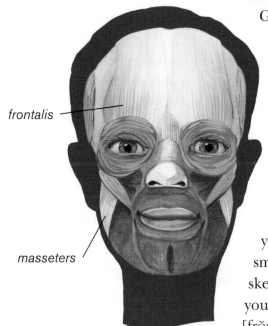

frontalis

masseters

The muscles that make up most of your arms, legs, abdomen, chest, neck, and face are called **skeletal muscles** because they are connected to your skeleton. Whenever you wrinkle your forehead, smile, or open and close your eyes, you are using some skeletal muscles—your **facial muscles.** The muscle on your forehead that raises your eyebrows is the **frontalis** [frŏn·tăl′ĭs]. When the frontalis is contracted, or tightened, for a long time, it can cause you to have a headache. If you put your fingers on your cheeks and clench your teeth, you can feel the **masseters** [mə·sē′tərz], which extend from your cheekbones down to your chin. Their job is to raise your lower jaw.

When you shrug your shoulders and move your head, you are using other skeletal muscles—one of which is the **trapezius** [trə·pē′zē·əs]. If you put your right hand on your left shoulder above the clavicle (collarbone) and swing your left arm, you can feel your trapezius muscle. Can you feel the top of the scapula (shoulder blade) with your fingertips? The trapezius is a large, triangular-shaped muscle which helps move the scapula.

Now put your left hand around your right upper arm and bend your elbow as you raise the lower part of your arm. The large skeletal muscle that you feel with your fingers is called your **biceps** [bī′sĕps′]. Your left thumb will be touching your **triceps** [trī′sĕps′].

Strong skeletal muscles cover your abdomen. These are your **abdominal muscles.** Your legs also have strong skeletal muscles. While you are sitting down, place your hand in the middle of your upper leg. As you raise and straighten your lower leg, you can feel your **quadriceps** [kwŏd′rĭ·sĕps′]. The muscles in the back of your thigh (upper leg) are called **hamstrings.** The hamstring muscles allow you to bend your knees and straighten your thighs. The quadriceps and hamstrings are used mainly for walking, kicking, and climbing.

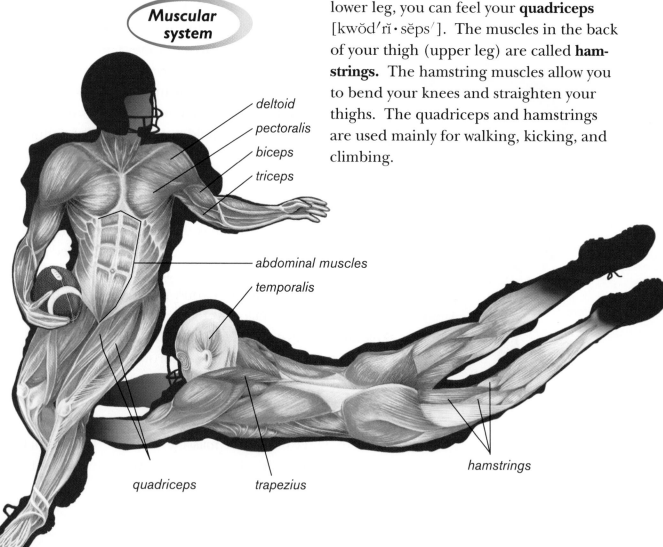

**Muscular system**

deltoid

pectoralis

biceps

triceps

abdominal muscles

temporalis

quadriceps

trapezius

hamstrings

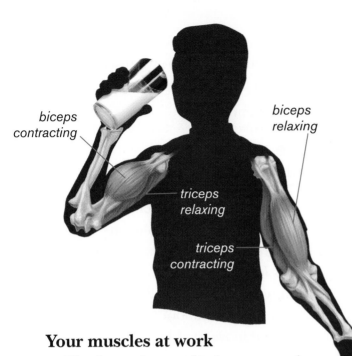

biceps
contracting

biceps
relaxing

triceps
relaxing

triceps
contracting

**work in pairs,** each movement usually involves two muscles. One muscle relaxes while the other one tightens, or contracts. When a muscle contracts, it gets shorter and thicker; when it relaxes, it gets longer.

**Each muscle always does its work by pulling; it never pushes.** Therefore, the muscle which bends your arm cannot straighten it. When you want to bend your elbow to take a drink of milk, your brain sends a message through your nerves to your biceps saying, "Biceps, contract." Your biceps contracts, and at the same time your triceps relaxes. Your biceps pulls on the tendon that is connected to your lower arm bone, and the tendon pulls the arm bone up. Because your triceps relaxes gently, it keeps the glass of milk from hitting you in the mouth. To lower the glass of milk, the triceps contracts, while the biceps relaxes gently to keep the glass from smashing onto the table.

## Your muscles at work

The bones in your body are moved by skeletal muscles. Most of the skeletal muscles are connected to bones by strong, white fibers, or cords, called **tendons.** In order for most skeletal muscles to function, both ends of the muscle must be connected to the bone. Since **most of the skeletal muscles**

## Your nerves work, too

Some nerves carry messages *to* your brain and spinal cord. Other nerves, called **motor nerves,** carry messages *from* your brain and spinal cord to your muscles. Whenever a nerve is damaged, it takes much time for it to repair itself. Therefore, if a motor nerve is cut or injured, the muscles that it serves may be paralyzed (unable to move) because your brain cannot send a message to the muscle telling it to contract. If the motor nerve dies, the paralysis will be permanent because a nerve can never be replaced.

The design of your brain, nerves, skeletal muscles, tendons, and bones allows you to walk, run, skate, swim, ride a bicycle, throw and catch a ball, and do many other things you wish to do. Because you can make your *skeletal muscles move when you want them to,* they are sometimes called **voluntary muscles.**

### Quick Checkup

1. Approximately how many muscles are in your body?

2. Name and describe your two kinds of facial muscles.

3. Identify the muscle (or muscles).
   a. They're connected to your skeleton.
   b. It helps move your scapula.
   c. It's on the front of the upper leg.

4. Are triceps on the top or bottom of your upper arm?

5. What are tendons?

6. What carry messages from your brain and spinal cord to your muscles?

7. What skeletal muscles move when you want them to?

## Some muscles are involuntary

Some of the most important muscles of your body are called **involuntary muscles.** *You cannot control the movement of these muscles.* They are moved by nerves which function automatically; thus you never have to think about them. The muscles that move food, liquids, and blood through your body are involuntary muscles. These include the muscles in your veins, arteries, stomach, and intestines. Most involuntary muscles contract and relax more slowly and rhythmically than the skeletal muscles. You can move the skeletal muscles in your arm back and forth very rapidly, whereas one contraction of your stomach muscles may last more than twenty seconds. Some involuntary muscles also allow your organs to change in shape and size as they do their work. You cannot

**The cardiac muscle at work**

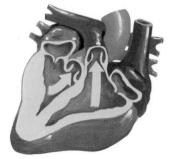
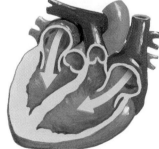

see the action of most of the involuntary muscles in your body—they work continuously without your being aware of them.

A very important involuntary muscle is your heart, or **cardiac muscle,** which is a large, hollow muscle about the size of your fist. Each time your cardiac muscle contracts, or beats, blood is pumped to all parts of your body to keep you alive. Your heart contracts around ninety times a minute—more than 100,000 times each day! Could you remember to tell it to contract each time?

## Building strong muscles

Whenever muscles are used, some parts of the body wear out or are used up. God designed our bodies so that these worn-out parts can be repaired or replaced when you eat the right foods. Your muscles are made mostly of protein; therefore, for the growth and repair of muscles, your body uses foods that contain a lot of *protein,* such as *lean meats, fish, poultry, eggs, milk, buttermilk, powdered milk, yogurt, cheese, soybeans,* and *wheat germ.* Not enough protein in your diet can cause soft, flabby muscles.

Carbohydrates supply energy for your muscles to work. Good sources of **carbohydrates** include *fruits, vegetables, whole-grain bread and cereals, seeds, nuts, dried beans and peas,* and *honey.* Calcium, in addition to building strong bones, also allows your nerves to function properly. Remember that nerves tell your muscles to contract. A lack of calcium may cause a muscle to contract so suddenly that you feel a sharp pain, or **cramp.**

Muscles can also become soft and weak from insufficient (not enough) use. ***When muscles are exercised, or used, they grow firmer, larger, and stronger.*** Voluntary muscles are made up of thousands of fine, long threads called **fibers,** which are bundled together. When muscles are exercised regularly, the heart supplies them with more blood and nutrients to make thicker muscle fibers; therefore, the more your muscles are used, the stronger they become.

## Muscle tone is important

Many muscles in your body are seldom completely relaxed except when you are sleeping. They are gently pulling against each other most of the time. This steady

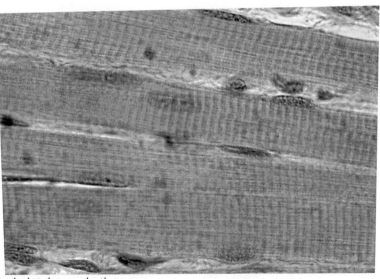

*skeletal muscle tissue*

contraction is called **muscle tone.** Muscles that are soft and flabby lack good muscle tone. Muscles that have good tone are firm and elastic; they respond quickly and easily when they are told to do something. As a result, they use less energy. Firm, elastic muscles are more easily trained to learn new skills for sports than soft, flabby muscles. If your muscles are firm, with practice you can coordinate them, or work them together, smoothly. Strength and coordination together make you skillful in an activity.

Because your muscles must work to hold your body in the proper positions for sitting, standing, and walking, good muscle tone is necessary for correct posture. If you have weak abdominal muscles, your back muscles must work harder to keep your

spinal column straight. Good muscle tone alone, however, will not keep your muscles strong. A variety of activities during work and play is necessary in order for you to use all of your muscles. Many skeletal muscles are used during active sports and games.

If you have poor muscle tone, you can damage your muscles by playing too long and too hard. When muscle fibers are stretched too far, they tear. Any damage to a muscle that causes pain is called a **strain.** Strained muscles can repair themselves with rest; however, most muscle strain can be prevented by keeping your muscles in good condition.

Sometimes muscle cramps are also caused by overworking little-used muscles. When a muscle cramps, the pain will not stop

until the muscle relaxes. Because skeletal muscles work in pairs, you can help a cramped muscle to relax by contracting the opposite muscle. If you have a cramp in the calf of your leg, the muscles on the front of your lower leg need to contract. Put your foot under something that does not move, or hold it down with your other heel, and try to lift your leg. In about twenty seconds, your calf muscle should be relaxed.

## Exercise builds endurance

Exercise does more for your body than just build strong skeletal muscles. Exercising rapidly will make your body more flexible, or **limber** (able to bend easily).

**Healthful** *Hint*

**Nothing ever comes to one, that is worth having, except as a result of hard work.**

*Booker T. Washington*

That's right.

Running, swimming, and jumping rope make your heart beat faster, and they fill your lungs with fresh air. These activities build your **endurance** (ability to keep on) by strengthening your heart and lungs as well as the skeletal muscles of your body. They help you to work and play longer without getting tired. When you stay active for fifteen or more minutes without rest, these activities are considered **aerobic** [â′rō′bĭk] exercises. Other aerobic activities that build your endurance include hiking, skating, playing basketball and soccer, and riding a bike.

Work is an excellent form of exercise. When you make your bed, vacuum the carpet, weed the garden, wash the car, rake the yard, and do other things to help at home, you not only are helping your muscles get exercise, but you are also helping your parents.

### Quick Checkup

1. Muscles which cannot be controlled are called __?__ muscles.
2. What is another name for your heart?
3. What are muscles mostly made of?
4. What is muscle tone?
5. Constant exercises of fifteen minutes or more are called __?__ exercises.

## Additional benefits from exercise

Any kind of exercise, whether working at home or playing an active game, helps to train your mind as well as your body. You store the knowledge of how to do new

It strengthens your bones and muscles.
It increases your endurance.
It improves your coordination.
It helps you to be flexible and agile.
It aids your body in producing blood cells.
It improves the circulation of your blood.
It aids your digestion.
It increases your energy.
It helps control your weight.
It improves your posture.
It helps you to relax.
It keeps you alert.

*Wow! Look at all the benefits of exercise!*

things in your brain. Exercise also rests your mind so that you can think better. Research shows that if you are active, you will do better work in school because you can concentrate and be alert for longer periods of time.

The blood, which carries food and oxygen to all parts of your body, circulates better when you exercise. Sufficient exercise improves your appetite and helps your body to digest and use the food you eat. It also helps your body get rid of waste materials. When you exercise regularly, your muscles, lungs, heart, and other organs work together more efficiently, and you are able to sleep better at night.

## Insufficient exercise is harmful

A lack of exercise causes waste materials to collect inside your body. Then your body parts do not function properly, and you feel tired and unhappy. Not exercising your lungs enough can cause you to have a flat chest and rounded shoulders. Not getting enough exercise can also cause your heart to become weak. A strong heart pumps more blood with each beat; therefore, it does not have to beat as often to do its work. For this reason, the heartbeat

**Question:** How does a hen stay so fit?
  **Answer:** She always does her eggsercises.

**Question:** What exercise can a snake not do?
  **Answer:** Toe touches.

of a well-trained athlete is much slower than an average person's heartbeat.

Exercise helps you to look healthier and to feel healthier. When you get up in the morning, or after you have been sitting still for a long time, exercise improves your circulation. You feel refreshed, and your mind is alert!

You probably have noticed that exercise makes you feel warm. This feeling of warmth is caused by an increase in the flow of blood to bring additional food and oxygen to the muscles. Before you begin any active game or vigorous exercise, you should warm up to prepare your skeletal muscles, your heart, and your lungs for

**EXERCISE 4 FITNESS**

## Curl-ups

This warm-up exercise will strengthen your abdominal muscle as it stretches and tones the muscles along your spine. Remember that a strong abdomen will help you to maintain good posture. Lie on your back with your knees bent and your arms at your sides. Slowly lift your head and shoulders as you reach for your knees. Hold this position for six seconds; then roll down, pressing the small of your back against the floor. Begin by doing six Curl-ups, and add a few more each day until you are doing twenty.

more strenuous exercise and thus prevent injury. Exercises such as slow stretches, arm circles, push-ups, and jumping jacks are good warm-up exercises. Such exercises—often referred to as **calisthenics**—also help build up the strength and endurance of your skeletal muscles. Activities such as the high jump and the long jump demonstrate the strength of skeletal muscles.

The most commonly used exercises for building muscular strength are calisthenics and weight lifting. You probably do some calisthenics during your physical education class, but you should not lift weights. Heavy weight lifting or power lifting is harmful for your body while you are still growing. It can cause back injuries and injuries to your bones, because the

## EXERCISE 4 FITNESS

### Side Benders

Standing with your feet apart and your elbows out, clench your fists above your shoulders. On the count of one, stretch out your arms and bend to the right. On the count of two, return to the starting position. On the count of three, stretch out your arms and bend to the left. On the count of four, return to the starting position again. Begin by doing five Side

Benders and gradually work up to twenty. This warm-up exercise will stretch the side muscles at your waist and hips and will help condition your upper arms. If you want to strengthen your upper arms, hold a two-pound weight in each fist as you do Side Benders. *Exercises that are done slowly, but with effort, will help make your muscles strong.*

bones of your spinal column and limbs (arms and legs) are not fully developed. Tasks such as hoeing weeds in the garden, raking the yard, carrying groceries, or pulling a younger brother or sister in a wagon will also help to strengthen your muscles.

Another way to exercise your muscles is by pulling or pushing hard against an object that does not move or against another part of your body. Such exercises are called *isometrics* [ī′sə·mĕt′rĭks].

Isometric exercises may be used to strengthen muscles. Abdominal muscles need to be strong to aid in lifting and in maintaining posture. Strength is also needed for muscles to avoid sprains or strains. Isometrics, however, will not build your endurance.

## Quick Sprints

This warm-up exercise will help you develop an **agile** [ăj′əl] body—a body that *moves quickly and easily.* Squat down and lean forward with both hands on the ground. Your fingers should be pointed forward and slightly spread apart. On the count of one, stretch out your right leg behind you. On the count of two, put your left leg backward and bring your right foot up by your hands. Keep your head up as you change the position of your feet quickly and smoothly. Begin by doing ten Quick Sprints, and work up to twenty-five.

## Muscle Maker

Try this exercise and see if you can determine which muscles it will strengthen. Put your hands together with your left hand on top of your right hand. Keeping your hands close to your chest, inhale and push your hands together as hard as you can while you count to six. Then exhale and let both arms relax at your sides. Next, reverse the hand positions by putting your right hand on top of your left hand. Inhale and push hard as you count to six; then exhale and let your arms relax again. Repeat the exercise five times. Which muscles did you feel contracting as you did the exercise? Could this exercise also be titled *Biceps Builder?*

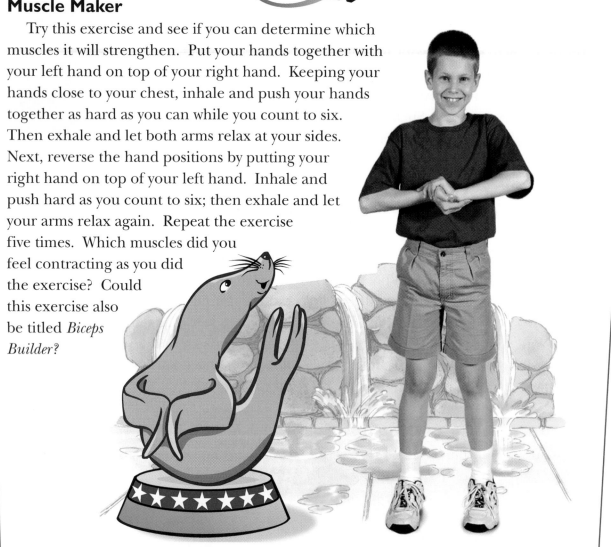

# Chapter Checkup

A. Study the muscular system diagrams on pages 21–22.

B. Identify each muscle.
1. a muscle at the back of the upper arm
2. a muscle at the front of the upper arm
3. a facial muscle that raises the eyebrows
4. a muscle which extends from the cheekbone to the chin
5. a large skeletal muscle which moves the scapula
6. an involuntary muscle
7. the muscle in the front of the upper leg
8. the muscles in the back of the upper leg

C. Define each term.
1. aerobic exercise
2. strain
3. cramp
4. endurance
5. limber
6. muscle tone
7. tendon

D. Answer each question.
1. How are all movements in your body made?
2. How many muscles are in the human body?
3. Why do most skeletal muscles work in pairs?
4. How can muscles be made stronger?
5. What attaches the skeletal muscles to the bones?
6. Why are skeletal muscles also referred to as voluntary muscles?

E. List five benefits of regular exercise.

# Your Breathing Machine

# chapter 3

"And the Lord God formed man of the dust of the ground, and breathed into his nostrils the breath of life; and man became a living soul" (Gen. 2:7). Breathing, which began with God's own breath, continues every minute of your life. Breathing, or **external respiration,** *is the process by which air enters and leaves your body.* An important gas found in the air you breathe is **oxygen.** Insufficient oxygen can cause illness or even death. Because your body can hold only a small amount of oxygen—enough to last less than three minutes—you must continually take in oxygen. Every part of your body needs food and oxygen to keep it alive and able to do its work. Your blood carries digested food, along with oxygen, to all parts of your body.

When your body breaks down food for heat and energy, a waste gas called **carbon dioxide** is given off. Your blood carries this waste to your lungs, and it is removed from your body when you exhale (breathe out). The oxygen that you inhale (breathe in) is joined to other food wastes to make water. Some of this water is used by the blood, and some of it is removed from the body as waste.

## Fresh air and sunshine

When you are active, you take quick, deep breaths to get the extra oxygen your body needs. Since fresh air contains the most oxygen, whenever possible you should exercise

**Question:** If you breathe oxygen during the day, what do you breathe at night?

**Answer:** Nightrogen.

where the air is fresh. Outdoor exercise gives you both fresh air and sunshine that your body requires. Since sunshine helps the skin to manufacture vitamin D in your body, vitamin D is sometimes referred to as the **sunshine vitamin.** It is very important for you to have sufficient vitamin D as your body grows because vitamin D helps your body absorb calcium to build strong bones and teeth.

Fresh air and sunshine bring a rosy color back to your cheeks after you have been sick. Just being outside in fresh air makes you glad to be alive—you want to work and be active. With sufficient fresh air, you also do better work at school because fresh air helps keep your mind alert. In cold winter weather when you stay inside most of the day, fresh air can prevent a tired and unhappy feeling. If you breathe stale air over and over, you may get a headache. A room filled with cool, moist, and circulating (moving gently) air makes you feel comfortable.

## Quick Checkup

1. What do we call the process by which air enters and leaves your body?
2. What important gas do you inhale?
3. What waste gas do you exhale?
4. What vitamin does your skin manufacture from sunshine?

## Your air conditioner

When you inhale, air is drawn through your nostrils or mouth. Breathing through your nose is healthier than breathing through your mouth because your nose cleans, moistens, and warms or cools the air as it enters your body. Hairs inside the nostril openings strain out dirt and dust as you inhale. Inside the nose, the nasal passages have a moist lining—the **mucous membrane**—which gives off a sticky fluid called **mucus.** The mucous membrane extends to the mouth, throat, inner ear, bronchial tubes, and lungs.

In the front of your skull you have four pairs of cavities (hollow places) called **sinuses.** The sinuses, which open into the nasal passages, are also lined with a mucous membrane. Mucus draining from the sinuses helps to moisten the nasal passages and thus helps moisten the air that you breathe. Some dust, pollen, and pathogens [păth′ə·jənz], or germs, that get past the hairs in the nostrils also cling to the mucus. Along the surface of the mucous membrane in the air passageways, tiny hairlike forms called **cilia** [sĭl′ē·ə] wave back and forth in rhythm to help filter more dust and pathogens from the air you breathe. Some dust and dirt is removed from your nose when you exhale; some is swallowed and is destroyed by acid in your stomach.

Many tiny blood vessels filled with blood are in the mucous membrane. This blood warms or cools the air that passes through your nose. The longer air takes to move through the nasal passages, the closer the air becomes to your body temperature. Every time you exhale, some of the air remains in your nose, and when you breathe in, the outside air mixes with this air. The hair and mucus also slow down the movement of air through the nasal passages. Your nose is so well designed for its work that the air is almost at body temperature before it enters your lungs. Because your nose filters the air which passes through it and also warms or cools the air, your nose can accurately be referred to as your air conditioner.

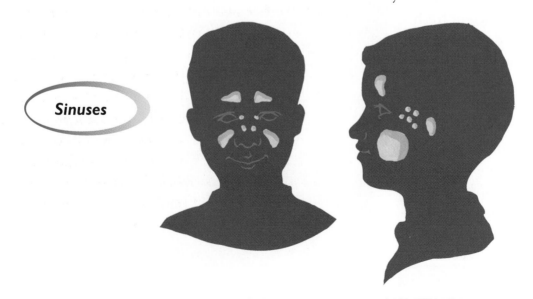

*Sinuses*

# Preventing infectious diseases

You should breathe through your mouth only when you cannot get enough air through your nose. A cold can make the mucous membrane in your nose swell so much that you have to breathe through your mouth. Every time you are running or playing hard, you automatically breathe through your mouth in order to get the extra air you need. Whenever you breathe through your mouth, dust is not filtered out, and because air enters your body so quickly, the air is not warmed as it is when it passes through the nasal passages. Cold air and dust that enter the throat cause the mucous lining of the mouth and throat to become dry. If you constantly breathe through your mouth, you are more likely to catch a cold, a sore throat, or an infectious disease.

Dust and pathogens caught in the mucus are blown out when you sneeze or blow your nose. Colds are most often caught by rubbing your nose or eyes after you touch something which has been touched by the hand of someone who has a cold and who has just touched his nose or used his hand to cover a sneeze. Whenever possible, catch a cough or sneeze in a tissue or hankie. Always use a clean hankie or tissue, and be sure you throw used tissues in a wastebasket or container. You should not try to stifle or hold back a sneeze by clenching your jaws shut or by holding your nose, since this can damage the mucous membrane. When you

blow your nose, blow gently through both nostrils at the same time to prevent pathogens from being forced into your ears.

Infections of the nose can spread easily to the sinuses, causing sinus trouble, or **sinusitis** [sī′nə•sī′tĭs]. In sinusitis, the mucous membranes in the sinuses become swollen, preventing air from entering the sinuses and the thickened mucus from draining out. When this happens, intense pain builds up in the sinuses, and the infected side of the face may swell. Sinusitis is harmful because the infection can spread to other parts of the body.

## Helpful infection fighters

Your **adenoids** [ăd′n·oidz′], located at the back of the nasal passage, and your **tonsils,** located at the back of your mouth, collect many harmful pathogens that might otherwise cause infections in your body. Sometimes there are so many pathogens that the tonsils and adenoids cannot destroy them all. Then your tonsils or adenoids may become infected. Without your tonsils and adenoids to destroy harmful pathogens

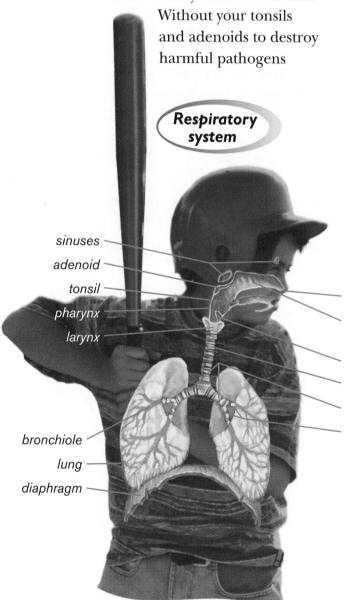

*Respiratory system*

sinuses
adenoid
tonsil
pharynx
larynx

nostril
nasal passage
epiglottis
trachea
bronchi
bronchial tubes

bronchiole
lung
diaphragm

which enter your nose or mouth, diseases would be more likely to enter your lungs.

## Pathway to your lungs

Using the diagram at the left, trace the route of air as it is inhaled or exhaled. After air is inhaled through your nose or mouth, it enters your throat, or **pharynx** [făr′ĭngks]. The pharynx opens into two passages—one for air and one for food. A tiny flap of cartilage called the **epiglottis** [ĕp′ĭ·glŏt′ĭs] covers the opening to the windpipe, or **trachea,** and prevents food and water from going into it. The epiglottis automatically opens when you breathe and closes when you swallow. If you try to swallow while you are talking or laughing, you may swallow a little food or water the "wrong way," or into the trachea. Your **larynx** [lăr′ĭngks], or voice box, located at the upper end of the trachea just below the epiglottis, is your final defense to keep food and water from entering your lungs. If food or water reaches the larynx, the vocal cords that are stretched across the larynx close off the trachea, and you cough violently until the food or water is expelled.

At its lower end, the trachea divides into two branches called **bronchi** [brŏng′kī]. One branch (bronchus) goes to each lung. Inside your lungs, the bronchi divide into many tubes called **bronchial** [brŏng′kē·əl] tubes. These tubes resemble an upside-down tree with branches that get smaller and smaller. The smallest tubes, called **bronchioles** [brŏng′kē·ōlz′], end in tiny air sacs. There

Breathe only through your nose unless it is impossible to do so or unless you need extra air.

are millions of these air sacs, or **alveoli** [ăl·vē′ə·lī], that expand like tiny balloons to hold air when it is breathed into the lungs.

## Quick Checkup

1. What do we call the moist lining of the nasal passage?

2. What is the sticky fluid produced by the mucous membrane called?

3. Name the four pairs of cavities (hollow places) in the front of your skull.

4. What is the name for the hairlike structures along the surface of the mucous membrane in the air passages?

5. What is another name for
   a. your throat?   b. your windpipe?
   c. your larynx?

6. Name the tiny flap of cartilage that covers the trachea during swallowing.

7. What are the two branches at the lower end of the trachea called?

8. What are the millions of tiny air sacs in the lungs called?

## The breathing muscle

Your ribs, sternum (breastbone), and vertebrae form the rib cage, which protects your heart and lungs. The top of each lung is up behind your clavicle (collarbone). Below the rib cage is your **diaphragm** [dī′ə·frăm], a flat sheet of skeletal muscle which separates the chest cavity from the abdominal cavity.

Breathing, like all of your body actions, is directed by nerves. They send out messages to the diaphragm and the muscles of the chest. When your diaphragm contracts, it moves downward, and at the same time your chest muscles lift your ribs up and out. This causes your chest to expand, and air containing oxygen rushes into your lungs. As the diaphragm relaxes, it moves upward, and your ribs

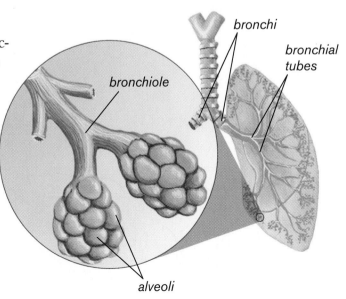

bronchi

bronchial tubes

bronchiole

alveoli

move down into place. This makes your lungs get smaller again, and some of the air is squeezed out of them. Regular breathing takes place as the diaphragm contracts and relaxes. When you are awake, you usually breathe more than fifteen times in one minute; you breathe less often when you are asleep.

The nerves which usually direct the process of breathing are controlled by the brain—but not the part of the brain you use for thinking. Thus, you can inhale and exhale air without thinking about it. Could you remember to breathe every three or four seconds? Try inhaling and exhaling every four seconds as you talk—your speech will be very choppy and difficult to understand. Since you have some control over your respiration, you can talk, sing, and laugh. If you could not hold your breath and let it out as needed, you could not do any of these because speaking, singing, and laughing can take place only as you exhale. Try reciting your address or telephone number as you inhale.

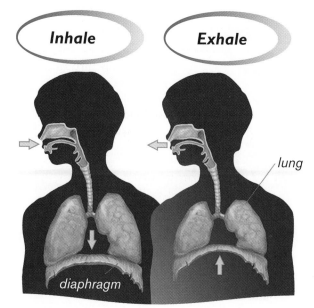

Inhale          Exhale

lung

diaphragm

The diaphragm contracts and moves downward.

The diaphragm relaxes and moves upward.

Could anyone understand you, or did you just make noise?

You normally inhale and exhale about one thousand times in one hour. If you breathe in about one pint of air every time you inhale, how many gallons of air would you breathe in and out in one day?

## Keeping your lungs healthy

Your lungs, which look like pink sponges, are elastic and can expand or contract according to the pressure surrounding them. They act as temporary storehouses for the air you inhale. This air is exchanged as you breathe in and out. From the air that you inhale, oxygen passes

16 gallons, 17 gallons, 18 gallons . . .

MILK

through the thin walls of the alveoli (air sacs) into the blood. At the same time, carbon dioxide, a waste gas, passes from the blood into the alveoli and is breathed out along with unused parts of the air when you exhale. *Exchanging oxygen and carbon dioxide between the air and the blood is the major purpose of the respiratory system.*

Your lungs need room to work. If one healthy human lung with its millions of expandable alveoli were spread flat, its surface area would cover a tennis court. Good posture makes it possible for you to breathe easily, because it allows your lungs to expand. When your posture is poor, your lungs are crowded, and they do not have enough room to work properly. Then your body does not get as much oxygen as it needs.

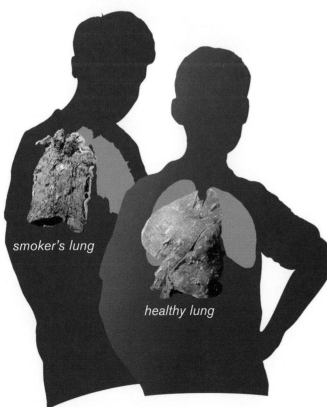

smoker's lung

healthy lung

One of the worst things a person could do to his lungs is to smoke tobacco. Smoking is a harmful habit that irritates the nose and throat and often causes coughing. Medical studies show that some of the most harmful effects of smoking concern the trachea, bronchial tubes, and lungs. Smoking paralyzes the cilia along the surface of the mucous membrane. When the cilia cannot filter the air, many pathogens that are inhaled enter the lungs. One of the substances in cigarettes—nicotine—is a poison that is used to kill insects. Whenever a person smokes, poisons from the smoke collect and seep through the blood vessels of the alveoli and are carried to all parts of the body. The more cigarettes a person smokes, the more poison enters his body, and the greater the harmful effects. As impurities enter the lungs, the lungs change from a pinkish color to a dark gray. Smoking can cause so many impurities to collect in the lungs that many of the alveoli cannot expand with air. Then the lungs cannot hold enough oxygen, and the person becomes short of breath. He cannot do strenuous work or participate in active sports because his body cannot take in the additional oxygen that it needs. The worst disease that is caused by smoking is **lung cancer.**

Alcohol may also weaken and injure the lungs by causing the blood vessels in the alveoli to become larger and thicker. Then oxygen cannot pass through the walls of the alveoli to the blood as fast as it needs to.

# Becoming physically fit

Regular vigorous exercise improves your respiration and helps your lungs to eliminate body wastes. When you are involved in strenuous work or play, you breathe faster and more deeply. The faster you breathe, the faster fresh oxygen reaches your body, and the faster the extra carbon dioxide is removed. Breathing deeply helps to keep your lungs strong and healthy; it strengthens the muscles which are used in breathing and helps them to fill your lungs with air.

Your physical fitness can be determined by how you feel when you get up in the morning or by how you feel at the end of the day. If you feel tired, you may need more rest, or you may need to improve your fitness. Physical fitness helps you do active things every day.

## Quick Checkup

1. What is the flat sheet of skeletal muscle which separates the chest cavity from the abdominal cavity called?

2. What waste gas is removed from your lungs?

3. What is the main purpose of the respiratory system?

4. What is the worst disease caused by smoking?

**Tickle Your FUNNY Bone**

**Question:** How does a tick get exercise?
**Answer:** It does acrobaticks.

**Question:** Which animal doesn't do all its exercises?
**Answer:** A cheetah.

**Question:** Where does a three-thousand-pound hippo do its exercises?
**Answer:** Anywhere it wants.

## Activity without rest

Swimming, jogging, cycling, rowing, jumping rope, and active sports, such as soccer and basketball, are called **aerobic** [â·rō′bĭk] exercises because they help your lungs to use more air with less effort. Your muscles need oxygen to do their work. When your muscles work hard, your body uses a large amount of oxygen. An aerobic exercise indicates the condition of your lungs to take in extra oxygen and the condition of your heart to deliver the extra oxygen to all parts of your body. Remember that aerobic exercises also build fitness and endurance because they use your large skeletal muscles for a long period of time.

Exercising now and then will not help build fitness, nor will it strengthen your heart and lungs. *Aerobic exercise gives your body continuous activity without rest periods. Fifteen or more minutes of aerobic exercise at least three times a week are needed to keep your body in good physical condition.* If you are in poor condition now, you will need to build up gradually. While you are in school, you can work on fitness during physical education class as well as before or after school and on Saturdays. During the summer months, you will have more time for vigorous work outside. You may also enjoy swimming, rowing, cycling, or playing active games with your family or friends.

Swimming is an excellent aerobic exercise because it exercises the muscles of both your upper and lower body. Since swimming causes less stress or strain on your joints and bones than running, you may be able to swim while you have some injuries.

## Warming up is important

*Before you begin a strenuous game or an aerobic exercise, your body needs to warm up gradually.* Light exercise speeds up the

work of your heart and lungs and gets them ready for more strenuous exercise. Your skeletal muscles also do better work when they are warm. These light exercises could include stretching exercises, warm-up exercises, and walking or jogging. If you do aerobic exercises early in the morning, stretching exercises are especially important because your body is less flexible in the morning than it is later in the day. Try touching your toes at seven o'clock in the morning and again at noon. You will find it easier to touch your toes at noon. Toe touches, especially with your legs crossed, help stretch the tendons and hamstring muscles in your legs. Slowly bend over and hold your position for ten seconds. Repeat this stretch one or two times. You should not bounce or jerk vigorously while you stretch; this could cause you to overstretch a muscle and tear the fibers.

In ordinary walking, less than half of the muscles in your legs are used. To get the most benefit from walking, you need to walk as fast as possible with your arms swinging loosely at your sides.

When your posture is correct, your body has more strength; therefore, correct posture for running will help you to run faster. For a **sprint** (a short, fast run), you can run faster if you run on your toes. A swayed back or a pelvis that tilts forward can cause you to have ankle or knee pains as you run.

## Additional requirements for aerobics

As you work or play hard, various muscles in your body are contracting vigorously. As a result, your muscles need additional food and oxygen to provide extra energy. **Carbohydrates,** such as *fruits,*

*vegetables, breads,* and *cereals,* supply energy for your muscles to work. If you are very active, you can get an extra supply of energy from foods containing fats and oils. Some good sources of **fats and oils** include *cooking oil, fish oil, butter, margarine, mayonnaise, cheese, whole milk, egg yolk, nuts, peanut butter, seeds,* and *wheat germ.*

The process by which your body produces and uses energy from food is called **metabolism.** Exercise raises your rate of metabolism and makes you more alert, thus increasing your ability to do good work at school. Because vigorous activity raises the rate of metabolism for hours, early morning exercise is especially beneficial.

## Quick Checkup

1. What kinds of exercises help your lungs use more air with less effort?

2. What is the process by which your body produces and uses energy from food?

**Healthful Hint**

A thirst-quenching drink of tart fruit juice is the best quick-energy beverage.

## Warm-up Walk

Walk quickly for two or three minutes with your arms swinging at your sides. Continue walking while you raise your arms and clap your hands above your head ten times. Each time you clap, lower your hands again. While you continue to walk, shake your hands and arms rapidly for several seconds.

## Aerobic Jump

Jumping rope improves your circulation, your muscle strength, and, if you jump continuously for at least fifteen minutes three or more times a week, it improves your fitness by strengthening your heart and lungs. Unless you are in good physical condition, begin by jumping only two or three minutes or until you feel tired; do not jump until you are fatigued.

As with any skill, the more you practice the better you become, and thus the more times you can jump without missing a step. When you jump for several minutes, change to a different method of jumping every 100 jumps. Can you jump with both feet together? Alternating your left and right foot? Left foot only? Right foot only? Try skipping over the rope one foot at a time or try jumping with your arms crossed. You should work up to 70 or 80 jumps per minute for at least fifteen minutes. After you are in good physical condition, use a watch with a second hand to determine how long you can jump 100 jumps per minute without missing.

Study the picture of the respiratory system
on page 38 and then label the parts.

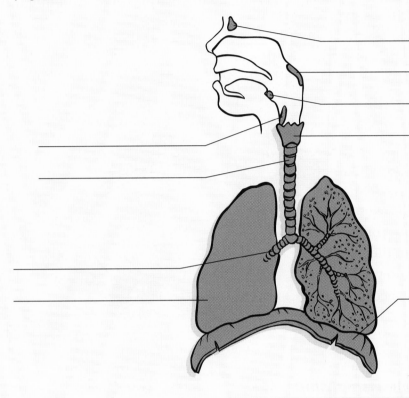

## Be a Good Sport

It takes a level head to win,
A level hand, a level eye.
But sometimes, even when you try
Your level best, things go awry.
You drop the ball, you miss your aim,
You slip a cog and lose the game.
Then comes the test. Don't make excuse;
Don't crumple; stand up in your shoes.
Remember, in a certain sense,
It takes a level head to lose!

—*Author unknown*

# Enjoying good sportsmanship

Part of the skill involved in playing an active game with others is your ability to play your own position and not interfere with the position of your teammates. ***Being a good sport includes learning to get along with others and learning how to work together.*** You learn to cooperate with others as you give your very best. As your team competes with another team, it is more fun to play if everyone follows the rules.

Self-control is another important part of good sportsmanship. When your team wins, it is natural for you to feel happy and excited; but you should also be considerate of the other team's feelings. How do you feel when you lose? Can you accept defeat gracefully? You should never try to make excuses for losing—no one likes to listen to a grumbler or complainer. You and everyone around you will feel better if, instead of grumbling, you smile and congratulate the players on the winning team.

Great game!

**Healthful Habits** *for good sportsmanship*

Play fair at all times.
Play for the joy of playing.
Do your best.
Follow orders.
Accept unfavorable decisions gracefully.
Play for the success of the team.
Do not be a quitter.

# Preventing possible injuries

After any strenuous exercise, you need to slow down and cool off gradually. Completely relaxing as soon as you finish exercising can cause you to feel dizzy or even faint. Putting on an extra sweater or jacket helps your body to cool off slowly. You should never go into a hot room or take a hot shower immediately after exercising. It is best to shower after you cool off and have stopped perspiring.

Although regular exercise is important, you should never exercise when you are sick or when you feel extremely tired. Overdoing aerobic exercise can cause muscle pain, exhaustion, and possible injuries. Instead of having more energy, you will continually feel tired.

Muscles are often strained when they are in poor physical condition. When your muscles are strengthened by exercise, the tendons which connect the skeletal muscles to the bones can be strained by exercising too long and too hard. The shoes you wear for jogging or running are important, too, because worn-down heels throw your feet off balance and may cause you to strain a tendon. Strained tendons can also be caused by running on hard surfaces with hard-soled shoes. Wearing good, cushion-soled shoes for running will help prevent ankle, foot, and leg problems.

The fitness and added alertness that you gain from aerobic exercises will also help you to avoid injuries. Exercising aerobically helps almost every process of the body—breathing, the circulation of blood, perspiration, eating, getting rid of wastes, and sleeping. Without sufficient exercise, your body cannot function as it should. Aerobic fitness will make you feel stronger and tire less easily. It gives you the ability to do the most activity with the least effort.

**Healthful Habits** *for physical fitness*

Warm up your body *before* strenuous activity. Cool your body gradually *after* strenuous activity. Do not exercise if you are sick or extremely tired.

Exercise outside whenever possible and get strenuous exercise 20–30 minutes at least three times a week.

# Chapter Checkup

A. Study the respiratory system diagram on p. 38.

B. Identify each part of the respiratory system.
1. the throat
2. the windpipe
3. the voicebox
4. a hollow cavity in the front of the skull
5. a tiny flap of cartilage that covers the entrance to the trachea
6. the muscle which separates the chest cavity from the abdominal cavity
7. air sacs inside the lungs
8. the moist lining inside the openings to the body
9. a sticky fluid produced by the mucous membrane
10. hairlike structures along the surface of the mucous membrane
11. two branches of the trachea that lead to the lungs
12. the two temporary storehouses for the air the body inhales

C. Answer each question.
1. What important gas in the air does the body inhale?
2. What waste gas does the body exhale?
3. What is the major purpose of the respiratory system?
4. What should you do before beginning any strenuous activity?
5. What does your body need to do after a strenuous activity?

D. Explain each concept.
1. Explain how good posture makes it possible for you to breathe easily.
2. Explain how aerobic exercises benefit your heart and lungs.

E. List five ways to become a good sport.

# A Winning Smile

Find a mirror and take a good look at yourself. Now, smile. A beautiful, healthy smile is meant to last a lifetime—and it can if you form good health habits while you are young. The small amount of time you spend daily on dental hygiene is an important investment in your future health, because healthy teeth and gums are necessary for good nutrition and thus are essential for good health.

## Purpose of teeth

Besides improving your personal appearance, your teeth also aid in clear speech. Do you remember when you were missing your primary incisors (front teeth)? You probably had difficulty saying such words as *safety* and *sorry* distinctly, because your teeth help you make the sound of *s, z, f, th,* and *j.* Say "thank you." Where do you feel your teeth when you make the *th* sound? Now, say "father." What two sounds in this word do your teeth help you make?

Another important function of the teeth is to prepare food for digestion. The different types of teeth cut, tear, grind, and crush solid food into tiny pieces. If the food is chewed well, **saliva,** *a digestive juice in the mouth,* mixes with it easily. Saliva begins the digestion of some foods. Saliva also moistens the food, making it easy to swallow.

# Structure of a tooth

Enamel covers the crown of a tooth—the part of a tooth that can be seen above the gum line. The enamel, which is *the hardest substance in your body,* protects the tooth from being worn away from the pressures of cutting, tearing, crushing, and grinding food. The **dentin** is a hard, bonelike tissue which forms and shapes the tooth. The **pulp,** the inner part of a tooth, contains nerves and blood vessels which enter the tooth through an opening at the tip of the root. A thin covering over the root, the **cementum,** holds the tooth firmly together. The **periodontal** [pĕr′ē·ə·dŏn′t′l] **membrane** is a layer of tissue between the cementum and the jawbone which connects the root of a tooth to the jawbone.

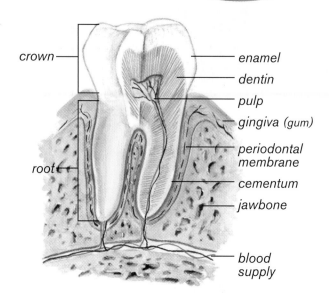

**A tooth's structure**

crown
enamel
dentin
pulp
gingiva (gum)
periodontal membrane
root
cementum
jawbone
blood supply

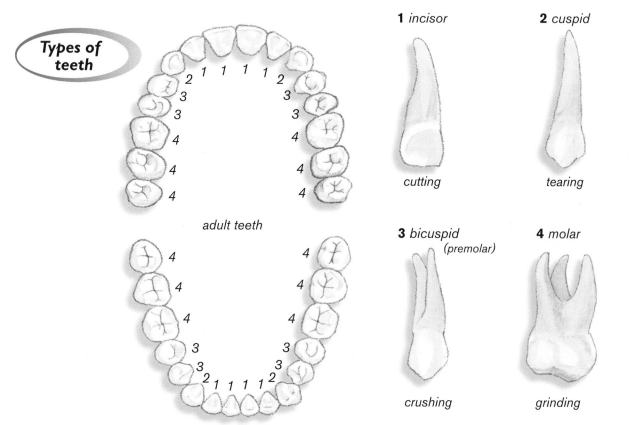

**Types of teeth**

adult teeth

**1** *incisor*

cutting

**2** *cuspid*

tearing

**3** *bicuspid* (premolar)

crushing

**4** *molar*

grinding

# The plaque attack

The teeth are one of the most durable parts of the body; however, your teeth are under continual attack, and thus they may not be healthy. Some 200 to 300 different kinds of helpful and harmful bacteria live in your mouth. **Plaque** [plăk], *a sticky, colorless film of harmful bacteria,* is constantly forming on and between your teeth. When sugar mixes with the plaque, tooth decay begins. Every time you eat something, plaque breaks down sugar in your mouth and changes the sugar to **acid;** the sticky plaque then keeps the acid on the surface of your teeth. Once the acid forms, it attacks the enamel on your teeth for about twenty minutes. After many acid attacks, the enamel is broken down, resulting in **dental caries** (commonly called cavities).

To help you understand the harm caused by an acid attack, place an uncooked egg in a clear glass and add enough vinegar (a mild acid) to cover the egg. After the egg soaks for six hours, observe what happens to the eggshell. Can the eggshell still protect the egg?

## Repeated acid attacks

*Sucrose, glucose, maltose, dextrose, lactose, fructose, corn sweeteners, natural sweeteners, molasses,* and *honey* are all forms of **sugar.** Most sugars—natural sugars or added sugars—mix with plaque and cause acid to form. It is not just *how much* sugar you eat that causes dental caries, however. *How often* you eat sugar and *how long* the sugar remains in your mouth also aid in the decay process.

Each time you eat sugar-rich foods, acid forms on your teeth. Thus, the more times you eat sugar-rich foods, the more times your teeth are attacked by acid. If you eat sweet foods between meals, you increase the number of acid attacks, and you increase the amount of acid in your mouth. When sugar-rich foods are eaten at mealtimes, the saliva, which is flowing readily by the end of a meal, helps to neutralize the acid.

## Quick Checkup

1. Define these terms.
   a. saliva    b. enamel
   c. dentin    d. plaque
2. What part of the tooth contains nerves and blood vessels?
3. What covers the root of the tooth?
4. What connects the root of a tooth to the jawbone?
5. What is sugar changed to when it is broken down by plaque?
6. When is the best time to eat sugar-rich foods?
7. What is another name for tooth decay?

## Lengthy acid attacks

Sweet foods that remain in your mouth a long time—including sugar-sweetened gum, breath mints, and cough drops—lengthen the acid attack. Sticky sweets such as mints, toffee and caramel desserts, raisins and other dried fruits, and peanut butter and jelly (or honey) sandwiches are extremely harmful if they are allowed to remain on your teeth. Acid could be attacking your teeth all day long.

Soft drinks of all kinds contain acid. If you drink many soft drinks a day or if you sip smaller amounts throughout the day, the acid will wear away your tooth enamel. You should not crack nuts with your teeth or bite hard objects, such as ice and hard candy, that could chip the enamel on your teeth. Biting thread with your teeth can also damage the enamel. When enamel is damaged or worn away, it cannot be replaced.

## The decay process

After a tooth has started to decay, it is difficult to keep the tooth clean. Pieces of food get into the decayed part and remain there even after the teeth are brushed, and thus the tooth continues to decay. When decay reaches the dentin, the decay process becomes more rapid. If decay reaches a nerve in the pulp, a toothache results.

A decayed tooth cannot rebuild itself. Once decay has begun, the tooth continues to decay until the decayed part is removed. Then a filling has to be put in.

## Effective plaque control

The saliva in your mouth helps promote good dental health by washing food from around your teeth and by neutralizing decay-causing acids in your mouth. By forming good daily habits to keep your mouth clean and free of plaque, you can prevent plaque attacks.

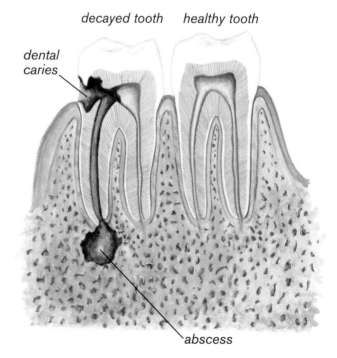

decayed tooth     healthy tooth

dental caries

abscess

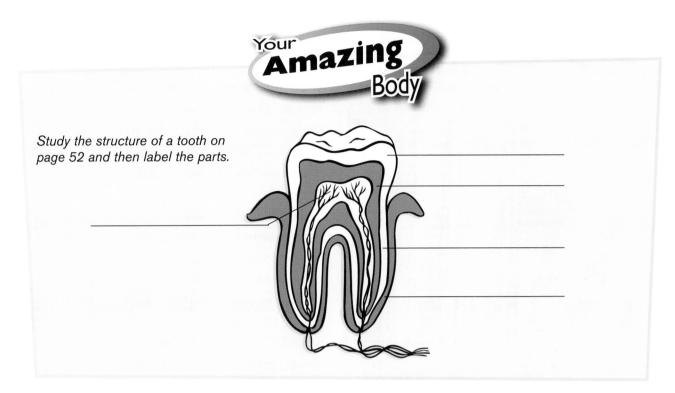

*Study the structure of a tooth on page 52 and then label the parts.*

## Brush frequently

There are several good methods for brushing your teeth, but the method you use is not as important as how well you brush. The next time you brush your teeth, time yourself with a watch that has a second hand. Were you finished brushing in less than one minute? If so, you probably removed no more than ten percent of the plaque from your teeth. That means ninety percent of the plaque remained to form acid for another plaque attack. Brushing your teeth thoroughly will probably take at least three minutes.

A flat toothbrush with medium-soft bristles helps remove food particles and

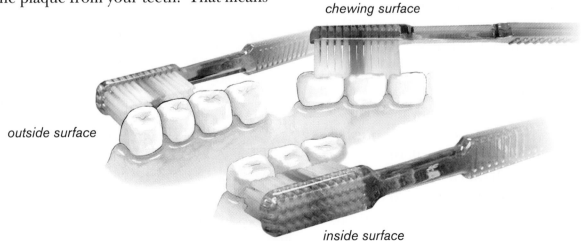

*chewing surface*

*outside surface*

*inside surface*

The time you spend daily on dental hygiene can ensure keeping your teeth for a lifetime.

plaque from your teeth; a brush that is too stiff may damage your gums. Your tooth-brush should be small enough so that you can reach every tooth. Always brush your teeth gently but vigorously and clean only one or two teeth at a time. Make sure you brush the inside, outside, and chewing surface of every tooth—upper and lower.

Be careful not to squash your tooth-brush, because only the tips of the bristles clean your teeth. A worn-out brush cleans poorly, and its bent bristles can injure your gums. You should replace your toothbrush usually every three or four months.

*Brush your teeth as soon as possible after you eat* to remove plaque and food particles. Whenever you cannot brush right after a snack or a meal, rinse your mouth well with water. Although the water will not remove plaque, it can wash away food particles which contain sugar.

Because plaque-producing bacteria are most active during the night, you should *brush your teeth again at bedtime.* The salivary glands release less saliva while you sleep than when you are awake. Thus, less saliva is available to help neutralize decay-causing acids in your mouth while you sleep.

Do you brush your tongue when you brush your teeth? You should—it helps to freshen your breath. Bacteria that grow in your mouth can cause bad-smelling breath, or **halitosis** [hăl′ĭ·tō′sĭs]. Breath-ing through the mouth is one cause of halitosis. Unpleasant-smelling breath can also be caused by some foods you eat or by an infection. Good oral hygiene usually will keep your breath fresh.

*Use a fluoride toothpaste* regularly to help prevent dental caries. Fluoride, which is absorbed by the enamel on your teeth, strengthens the enamel, making it more resistant to acid attacks. Put be-tween a half inch and an inch of fluoride

toothpaste on your brush each time to effectively fight tooth decay.

Always rinse your toothbrush thoroughly with running water each time you use it. Because harmful bacteria can multiply rapidly on a moist toothbrush, you should keep your toothbrush in a clean place where the air can surround it and dry it.

### Quick Checkup

1. When should you brush your teeth?

2. When are plaque-producing bacteria the most active?

3. What do we call bad-smelling breath?

## Floss daily

Most plaque forms near the gum line and between your teeth where your toothbrush cannot reach; therefore, much plaque remains on your teeth even after you do a thorough job of brushing them. Flossing removes the plaque and food particles from these areas where tooth decay and gum disease often start; thus you should *floss your teeth at least one time every day* before you brush them. Remember that while you sleep, less saliva is produced to help neutralize decay-causing acids. Flossing your teeth at bedtime to remove plaque and food particles that produce acids helps protect your teeth and gums when your body's natural protection is lower.

Dentists recommend that most people use unwaxed floss or dental tape; however, if your teeth are crooked or crowded, you

may need to use waxed floss. If you do not regularly floss your teeth now, your gums may bleed and feel sore the first few days you floss them. As the plaque-producing bacteria are removed, your gums will heal and stop bleeding if they are healthy. If you stop flossing for a time, your gums may bleed when you begin again.

Floss that is used incorrectly can injure your gums. Always be careful when you insert it between your teeth and under the gum line; do not let the floss snap into your gums. To insert floss gently between your teeth, hold the floss tight with your thumbs and first fingers and use a gentle sawing back-and-forth motion. At the gum line, curve the floss into the shape of a *c* around one tooth. While holding the floss tightly against the tooth, move the floss away from your gum—down on the top teeth and up on the bottom teeth. Before removing the floss, curve it around the adjacent tooth. You should use clean floss between each set of teeth.

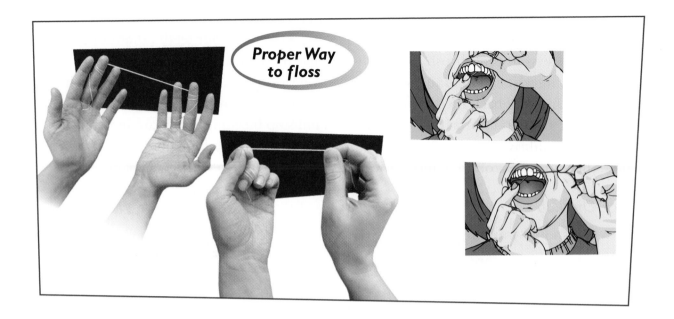

Proper Way to floss

Like any skill, flossing your teeth will take less time with practice. If you floss your teeth the same way each day and establish a regular time to floss them, flossing will soon become a good habit.

## Buildup of plaque

Plaque is even more harmful when it is allowed to remain on your teeth for twenty-four hours. If you do not remove plaque by daily brushing and flossing, the plaque builds up and forms a hard deposit called **calculus,** or tartar. A hardened deposit of calculus contains many pits and holes where bacteria multiply rapidly. Calculus extends down under the gum line and irritates the gums, causing them to pull away from the teeth. This pulling away leaves pockets that fill with food particles and plaque and thus more calculus.

When calculus accumulates, the gums become tender and inflamed. This infection causes the gums to bleed easily when

Tickle Your FUNNY Bone

Question: How does a tick clean its teeth?
Answer: With a tooth-tick.

Question: What does an alligator eat after its teeth are pulled?
Answer: The dentist.

Reduce sugar intake.

Brush frequently.
Floss daily.

the teeth are brushed. If the infection is left untreated, it can lead to a **periodontal disease** which infects the bones supporting the teeth. Remember that the periodontal membrane connects the root of a tooth to the jawbone. As the periodontal disease progresses, the jawbones supporting the teeth are destroyed; then the teeth loosen and move from their normal position. Eventually the teeth could even fall out.

Periodontal (gum) diseases often begin in childhood with the buildup of plaque and calculus when brushing and flossing are neglected. Because periodontal diseases usually progress slowly for many years with little or no pain, poor dental hygiene during childhood years often leads to future problems. Although periodontal diseases usually affect adults, they can occur at any age.

## Regular dental checkups

If plaque builds up on the teeth and forms calculus, the calculus cannot be removed with normal brushing and flossing. Only a dentist or **dental hygienist** [hī·jē′nĭst: dentist's assistant] can remove calculus from your teeth. Your dentist or dental hygienist may also instruct you on plaque control.

Your teeth should be cleaned about every six months, when your dentist also examines your teeth and gums for decay and disease. If you have any cavities, the dentist will remove the decayed part and put a filling in the tooth. After cleaning your teeth, your dentist may apply fluoride to them. Remember, fluoride strengthens your teeth and helps protect them against decay-causing acids.

Learn to recognize signs of periodontal disease:

Puffy, tender gums
Gums that bleed easily
Continual bad breath
Infection between the gums and the teeth
Gums that pull away from the teeth
Loose permanent teeth

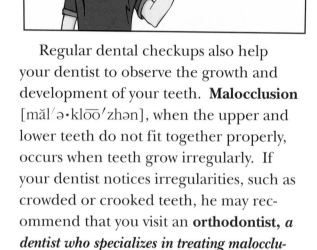

Regular dental checkups also help your dentist to observe the growth and development of your teeth. **Malocclusion** [măl′ə·klōō′zhən], when the upper and lower teeth do not fit together properly, occurs when teeth grow irregularly. If your dentist notices irregularities, such as crowded or crooked teeth, he may recommend that you visit an **orthodontist,** *a dentist who specializes in treating malocclusion.* An orthodontist often uses braces to move teeth gently into place. The process of straightening teeth may take months or sometimes years to complete.

Crowded, crooked teeth are difficult to clean, and they are more likely to decay than straight teeth. If the upper and lower teeth do not meet properly, it is difficult to chew food thoroughly. Thus, an untreated malocclusion can affect both the dental health and the general health of an individual.

## Treating injured teeth

Accidental injuries to the teeth can occur, especially during childhood. One or more teeth may be cracked, broken, or pushed out of alignment. When any injury to a tooth occurs, you should call your dentist immediately.

A permanent tooth that is knocked out in an accident can usually be saved if you know what to do. If the tooth is still in the mouth, gently push it back into the socket as far as it will go. If the tooth is on the 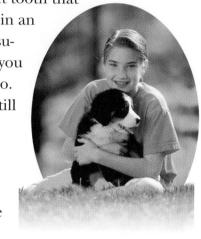 ground, pick it up by the crown; be careful not to touch the root of the tooth. Quickly—but carefully—rinse the tooth under slow-running water. The tooth should not be placed in mouthwash, alcohol, or any chemical, and it should not be scrubbed with anything hard or rough.

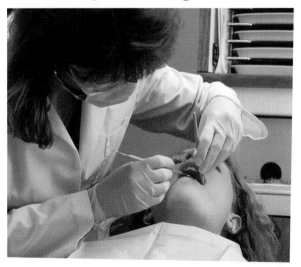

After the tooth is rinsed, place it in a cup of milk to keep it moist on the way to the dentist. The tooth could also be placed in the mouth between the cheek and the gum to keep it moist. Often a tooth that is replanted after an injury can reattach itself to the jaw and function normally. The sooner the dentist replants the tooth, the more likely its root is to reattach to the jawbone.

## Strong, healthy teeth

Clean, strong teeth are attractive, and they indicate both good dental hygiene and proper nutrition. A **balanced diet,** *a variety of foods containing all the nutrients necessary to keep you healthy,* is also necessary for healthy teeth and gums. Remember that if you eat between meals, you should snack on foods that contain little or no sugar, such as fresh vegetables, nuts, and cheese.

A poor diet can weaken the gums and the bones which support the teeth. Do your gums frequently bleed when you brush your teeth? Healthy gums do not bleed. Sufficient vitamin C, vitamin A, and the B vitamins from a balanced diet will help keep your gums healthy. Do you remember which mineral vitamin D helps your body to absorb in order to form strong bones? Your body also uses calcium to build strong teeth. Can you name a good source of this mineral? For other good sources of calcium, refer to the chart of nutrients on pages 10 and 11.

Because straight, healthy teeth improve your appearance, they help you to feel confident. Do not keep them hidden. Smile—a winning smile.

### Quick Checkup

1. What is a hard deposit of plaque called?
2. What disease affects the tissues and bones that support the teeth?
3. What is the improper fitting of the upper and lower teeth called?
4. What do we call a dentist who specializes in treating malocclusion?
5. What is a balanced diet?

## Soccer Tag

Soccer Tag can be played with a soccer ball on any playing area that has definite boundaries, such as a large circle or half a basketball court. Any number of players can play.

All players can move anywhere within the playing area, but they cannot go beyond the boundary lines except to recover the ball. One player is selected to be the *tagger,* and he must also stay within the boundary lines. Any player who goes beyond the boundaries receives a foul.

When the ball is rolled onto the playing area, the tagger runs and kicks the ball, trying to tag (hit) a player below the waist with the ball. If a player is tagged, he becomes the tagger. If the ball goes outside the boundary lines, the player closest to the ball gets it and rolls it back onto the playing area. A player can touch the ball with his hands only to recover the ball outside the boundary lines or to block the ball if it is above his waist. If he uses his hands at any other time, he receives a foul. The tagger receives a foul any time he kicks the ball higher than a player's waist.

All players begin the game with five points. Each time a player is tagged or receives a foul, he loses one point. When a player loses all five of his points, he is out and must stay outside the boundaries of the playing area. If a tagger loses his last point, he continues to play until he tags another player. The last player who remains inside the boundaries is the winner.

## Healthful Habits    for good dental hygiene

Eat a variety of foods for proper nutrition.

Eat sugar-rich foods only at mealtimes.

Brush your teeth as soon as possible after you eat.

Brush your teeth at bedtime.

Use a fluoride toothpaste.

Floss your teeth at least one time every day.

Have regular dental checkups.

# Chapter Checkup

A. Study the tooth's structure diagram on p. 52.

B. Define each term.
1. calculus
2. cementum
3. dental caries
4. dentin
5. enamel
6. malocclusion
7. orthodontist
8. plaque
9. pulp
10. saliva

C. Answer each question.
1. What is formed when sugar mixes with plaque?
2. When are plaque-producing bacteria the most active?
3. What causes halitosis?
4. What mineral is absorbed by the enamel on teeth, making the enamel more resistant to acid attacks?
5. When should you brush your teeth?
6. How often should you floss your teeth?
7. Why is it important to floss correctly?
8. What disease causes infection of the gums and the bones supporting the teeth?
9. If a tooth is knocked out, what part of the tooth should you not touch?
10. What is a balanced diet?

D. Explain how plaque attacks the teeth and how these attacks can be prevented.

# Your Body's Cover

# chapter 5

The skin that covers your body today is not the same skin you had last year. Your skin grows as you grow. To help you understand how large your skin is, measure the length of your arm and the distance around it. Cut a piece of paper this size for each arm. Measure the length and the distance around one of your legs and cut a piece of paper this size for each leg. Measure your head and trunk and cut pieces of paper to these sizes. Now lay the pieces of paper on the floor. If your skin were spread out flat, it would cover about this same area.

Like the rest of your body, the skin is made up of tiny parts called **cells.** Your skin makes millions of new cells each day to replace dead cells that are constantly being rubbed off. If your skin gets cut or burned, new skin grows to make your cover whole again. Your skin also regulates the temperature of your body, protects your body from injury, guards against pathogens (germs), helps heal cuts, helps remove wastes from your body, stores water and excess energy, and produces vitamin D.

# Your outer skin

Your skin, which God designed as a protection for your body, is made up of three layers. The *outer skin,* or **epidermis** [ĕp/ĭ·dûr′mĭs], contains no blood vessels. It is made up of twelve to fifteen layers of cells.

The lower cells in the epidermis are alive; they keep making new cells, which push the old ones upward. The cells become flatter and drier as they are pushed toward the surface of the skin. Tiny flakes of dead skin fall off when you wash, rub, scratch, or scrape your skin.

## Various thicknesses

Not all of your skin is the same thickness; in some places it is very thick—feel the skin on the palm of your hand. In other places your skin is very thin. Gently feel the skin on your eyelid or pinch the skin on the back of your hand. The parts of your skin that get the roughest treatment have the thickest epidermis. An extra thick, hard layer of epidermis called a **callus** develops when there is constant rubbing or pressure. A callus will go away

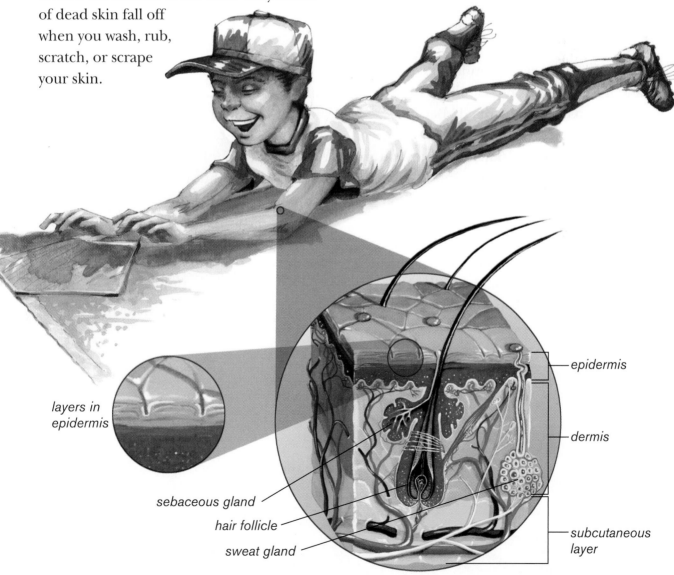

*layers in epidermis*

*epidermis*

*dermis*

*sebaceous gland*

*hair follicle*

*sweat gland*

*subcutaneous layer*

**Question:** Why does an elephant have wrinkled skin?

**Answer:** Did you ever try pressing one?

gradually when the rubbing or pressure is stopped.

Excessive rubbing may cause a **blister,** a raised part of epidermis that is filled with a watery substance. At first, the injured part of the skin is very tender and sore, and if the blister is not cared for properly, it can become infected. Because unbroken skin over a blister helps protect the deeper layers of skin from infection, you should try not to break most blisters. Carefully wash the skin around a blister with warm, soapy water, and then cover it with a sterile (free from pathogens) bandage. Bandages which are wrapped in paper are sterilized (made sterile) by heat. If the blister is broken, you should watch for **signs of infection—*redness, swelling, pus, and throbbing pain.***

A blister located where rubbing will continue, such as on a foot, should be opened and drained. After the blister is carefully washed, clean a needle with an **antiseptic** such as rubbing alcohol or hydrogen peroxide [hī′drə·jən pə·rŏk′sīd′]. An antiseptic destroys many pathogens and thus helps prevent infection. Prick one side of the blister with the sterilized needle and gently press the opposite side to force out the fluid. Do not remove the skin.

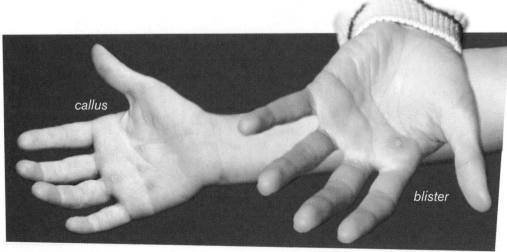

callus

blister

After the blister has been drained, cover it with a sterile bandage. While the epidermis slowly heals or is replaced, the tenderness disappears.

### Quick Checkup

1. What are the tiny parts that make up the skin called?

2. What is your outer skin called?

3. What is a thick, hard layer of epidermis called?

4. What do you call a raised part of your epidermis that is filled with a watery substance?

5. What are four signs of infection?

## Additional protection

Your hair and nails are also part of the epidermis. Your nails are hard and tough to protect the tips of your fingers and toes. The whitish, half-moon area at the base of a nail is part of the root from which new nail cells grow. As new nail cells form, the older cells are pushed outward and harden to form the nail. The ends of your nails are made up of dead cells; thus, when you trim your nails, you feel no pain because only dead nail cells are cut.

Your hair protects your body, too. It protects your head from heat, cold, and too much sun. Your eyebrows keep perspiration out of your eyes, and your eyelashes prevent dust and dirt from entering your eyes.

New cells at the root of each hair push the old cells toward the surface. As the old cells are pushed out, they die and form the hair that you see. Does it hurt when your hair is cut? Pull a few hairs on your arm. How do you know that the roots contain live cells?

## The color of skin

The lower part of the epidermis contains **pigments,** or *coloring matter,* which give your skin its color. A dark-colored pigment, **melanin** [mĕl′ə•nĭn], gives the skin a brownish color. People with light-colored skin have less melanin than people with dark skin. Another pigment gives a yellow color to the skin. The blood in small blood vessels showing through the skin adds a rosy color. This rosy color is particularly noticeable on your lips.

**Healthful Hint**

Before treating any injury, you should wash your hands thoroughly with soap and warm, running water.

Not all of your skin contains the same amount of melanin; therefore, some parts of your skin are darker than others. Do you have any freckles? Sometimes the melanin collects in little spots, making the spots darker than the rest of the skin. Being outside in the sunshine causes the melanin to build up and the skin to darken temporarily. This tanning of the skin is especially noticeable in white skin.

## The purpose of color

Skin color is one of God's special ways of caring for people. In areas close to the equator where it is extremely hot, the sun shines with direct rays, and thus the people are exposed to many **ultraviolet** [ŭl′trə·vī′ə·lĭt], or harmful, **rays** of the sun. When God scattered the people from the Tower of Babel "upon the face of all the earth" (Gen. 11:9), some of them settled near the equator on the continent of Africa. God provided these people with the ability to produce a large amount of melanin, making their skin very dark. The melanin in the epidermis helps prevent the sun's ultraviolet rays from harming the rapidly multiplying cells of the lower epidermis. The darker the skin color, the greater the amount of melanin, and thus the more protection the epidermis

gives from ultraviolet rays. People now living in North America whose ancestors were from Africa have inherited the ability to produce large amounts of melanin. Their dark skin is a testimony of God's provision for their forefathers.

The people who traveled from the Tower of Babel to the continents of Europe or northern Asia were far from the direct rays of the sun. Because they needed little protection from the sun, they had less melanin than people with darker skin; thus their skin was fair (light-colored). People with different skin colors have now spread to most parts of the world.

A few people—called **albinos** [ăl·bī′nōz]—have no pigment in their skin. Albinos have very light skin, white hair, and the colored parts of their eyes are pink. Because albinos have no protective melanin, they must be very careful to protect their skin and eyes from the sunlight.

## Your real skin

Much of your skin's work is done in *the layer of skin beneath the epidermis.* This layer of skin—the **dermis**—contains connective tissue, blood vessels, nerve endings, hair follicles, oil glands, and sweat glands. The connective tissue makes your skin elastic and strong; it also attaches your skin to your muscles. Blood vessels in the dermis carry food and oxygen to the new skin cells. When the dermis is cut, your skin bleeds, and you feel pain.

### The root of the hair

Hair grows on most parts of your body except on the palms of your hands and on the soles of your feet. The live cells, or root, of each hair grow in a little sac called a **hair follicle.**

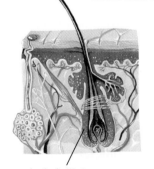

hair follicle

As long as the hair follicle is alive, a hair grows. Hair follicles sometimes die or are destroyed by disease, and baldness occurs.

Do you ever have "goose bumps"? There are little muscles at the root of every hair. If you feel cold or excited or are suddenly frightened, these tiny muscles contract, and the hairs stand straight up, causing goose bumps.

### Curly or straight hair

The texture and curliness of your hair are determined by the shape of the hair follicles. If the follicles are round and straight, the hair will be straight; if the follicles are flattened and curved, the hair

straight hair

wavy hair

curly hair

will be curly. The extent of the curl depends on the flatness and the curve of the follicle.

### Quick Checkup

1. What is the coloring matter that gives your skin its color called?

2. What is the dark-colored pigment that gives the skin a brownish color?

3. What are the harmful rays of the sun called?

4. What is the layer of skin beneath the epidermis called?

5. What is a hair follicle?

### The color of hair

The color of your hair is determined by the pigment that is deposited in new hair cells before they grow out of a follicle. Red hair contains an iron pigment that is not found in any other color of hair. As people grow older, pigment is no longer deposited in the new hair cells on the head; and the hair gradually loses its color. Tiny bubbles of air in the hair make it look white. A mixture of pigmented and unpigmented hair usually appears gray. Scientists have not yet discovered why hair loses its color.

## A layer of padding

Below the dermis lies the **subcutaneous** [sŭb′kyoo·tā′nē·əs] layer of skin—*a fatty layer that stores energy.* Like the epidermis, the subcutaneous layer varies in thickness from one place on your body to another. This fatty layer cushions your muscles and bones against shocks and jolts, and during cold weather, it helps hold in your body heat.

## Three layers of skin

Can you name the three layers of skin? A burn can affect one, two, or all of these layers. A **first-degree burn,** such as a mild sunburn or scald, affects only the epidermis, the outer, or *first,* layer of skin. The burned area appears red and feels painful, but there are no blisters, and the skin is not broken. For a first-degree burn, you should put the burned area under cool

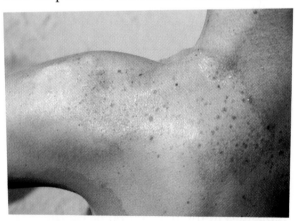

water immediately or apply a cold (not icy) wet cloth on it. If the pain continues, apply a first-aid cream or spray. *Do not put butter or grease on a burn,* because fats keep in the heat and increase the chance of infection. Butter also contains salt, which stings when applied to a burn.

A **second-degree burn,** such as a severe sunburn, burns through the epidermis into the dermis, the *second* layer of skin. Many burns caused by an electrical appliance or a boiling liquid are also second-degree burns. A second-degree burn forms blisters and feels extremely painful. If the blisters break, the skin appears wet and oozy. Like a first-degree burn, a second-degree burn should be put under cold water or have cold cloths applied to it immediately. You should gently blot the burned area dry and cover it with a dry, sterile bandage. Do not use cotton balls on a severe burn, because loose fibers may stick to the skin, causing an infection. *Try not to break the blisters,* because an open burn can become infected easily. Depending on the location of the burn and how large an area it covers, a second-degree burn may require medical treatment.

In a **third-degree burn,** the subcutaneous, or *third,* layer of skin is involved, and the entire thickness of skin is destroyed. The burned area may turn black or white.

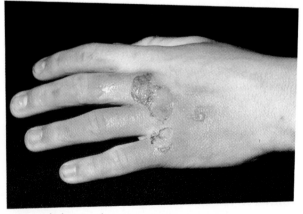

*second-degree burn*

Because nerve endings have been damaged or destroyed, there may be little or no pain. Anyone with *a third-degree burn needs emergency medical treatment.* Do not touch, clean, or apply any medication to a third-degree burn; and do not remove any clothing that sticks to the burn. If possible, cover the burned area with a sterile, nonstick bandage or pad or a clean cloth, such as strips of a clean sheet. Covering the burn will help prevent infection and will help relieve the pain, if any, by keeping oxygen from the burn.

## Your skin at work

### Preventing dryness

The dermis contains **sebaceous glands** (oil glands) which are connected to the hair follicles. The sebaceous glands produce an oily substance called **sebum.** Sebum, which is released through the hair follicles to the surface of the skin, spreads over the surface of the skin to keep it smooth and soft. This thin layer of oil that covers your entire body helps waterproof your body and prevents too much water from evaporating through your skin. If you stay out in the sun too long, your skin becomes dry because the sun dries the sebum faster than the dermis can make it. Wind also dries the sebum on your skin. If the skin does not have sufficient oil, it becomes so dry that it cracks.

### Controlling your temperature

Your skin contains two to three million **sweat glands,** which help your body to maintain a normal temperature of about 98.6 °F. Sweat glands are very plentiful

under your arms, on the palms of your hands, on the soles of your feet, on your back, and on your forehead. The sweat, or perspiration, travels from the sweat glands through tiny tubes leading to pores (tiny openings) in the epidermis.

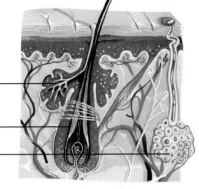

sebaceous gland

hair follicle

sweat gland

Although the sweat glands remove some wastes from your body, their main purpose is to cool your body as the perspiration evaporates. These glands never stop working. The perspiration usually evaporates into the air before it collects in drops;

however, on hot days or whenever you are involved in strenuous activity, large drops of perspiration often form on your skin. Sometimes when the weather is humid, perspiration collects on the skin faster than it evaporates. As a result, you feel hotter than on a less humid day.

The blood vessels in your skin help keep your body temperature normal, too. As food is broken down in your body, energy and heat are produced. Vigorous exercise also makes heat in your body. Some of this heat passes to the outside air through the blood vessels in your skin. When you get too warm, the tiny blood vessels in your skin expand so that more blood can flow into them. Some of the extra heat from the blood then passes through the skin to the outside air. Whenever your body gets cold, the blood vessels in your skin contract. Then less blood flows into the skin, and a smaller amount of heat passes through the skin to the outside air.

## Quick Checkup

1. Name the fatty layer of skin that stores energy.

2. How should each burn be treated?
   a. a first-degree burn
   b. a second-degree burn
   c. a third-degree burn

3. What type of burn affects
   a. the epidermis and dermis?
   b. only the epidermis?
   c. all three layers of skin?

4. What is another name for the oil glands in the dermis?

5. What is the oily substance that keeps the skin soft and smooth?

6. How does perspiration leave the body?

## Keeping out bacteria

Your skin normally has no openings except natural ones, such as your nose and mouth and the pores in the epidermis which lead to the sweat glands and the oil glands in the dermis. The skin is such an excellent covering for your body

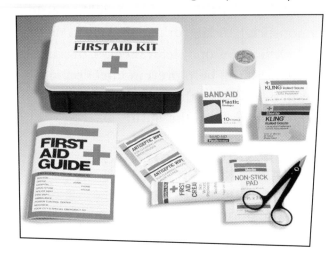

that it prevents disease-causing bacteria (pathogens) from getting into your body. Without the protection of your skin, harmful bacteria that are in the air and on every

object you touch would enter your body and kill you in just a few hours. Even a tiny break in your skin, such as a cut or a scratch, allows some harmful bacteria to enter your body. Do you remember what to do before treating any injury? After washing your hands thoroughly, you should clean the cut or scratch with soap and warm water. If the skin is torn, it can become infected easily, so be sure that the wound is cleansed well. An abrasion (scrape) should be cleaned with soap, warm water, and sterile cotton or gauze. Wipe the cotton or gauze from the center of the abrasion away from the wound to wash out dirt and pathogens. If possible, rinse a cut, scratch, or abrasion under running water. After rinsing the wound thoroughly, carefully blot it dry and cover it with a sterile bandage.

## Healing injuries

When you get a cut or a scratch, the blood vessels in the skin contract to stop the flow of blood. A clot of blood begins to form and fill the injury; platelets in the blood stick to each other and to both sides of the cut. Because the blood clot (scab) is a protection for the wound, you should not pick it off. As the blood clot shrinks, the two sides

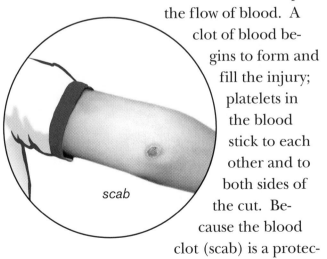

scab

of the cut are pulled closer together. Later, new skin cells growing from each side of the cut join together. A scar sometimes remains where the skin cells are joined.

## Producing vitamin D

Cholesterol is a substance which is manufactured in the liver and is normally found in the blood, brain, nerves, and skin. When ultraviolet rays of the sun shine on your skin, they change cholesterol in your skin into vitamin D. This is why vitamin D is sometimes called the *sunshine vitamin.*

Remember that God provided large amounts of melanin to the groups of people who would settle near the equator when mankind spread out from the

Tower of Babel. Because of this protection, these dark-skinned people could work long hours in the sun, producing sufficient vitamin D from the ultraviolet rays without causing overexposure to them. Dark-skinned people now living in colder climates, which lack the direct rays of the sun, often lack sufficient vitamin D. Anyone spending too little time in the sunshine cannot produce sufficient vitamin D for healthy teeth and bones. Such people must be sure to eat foods which contain this vitamin. For good food sources of vitamin D, refer to the chart of nutrients on pages 10 and 11. If you lack sufficient vitamin D, it will show in the structure of your teeth and bones. A lack of vitamin D can also cause **rickets,** *a disease in which the bones become weak,* causing irregular growth and deformities.

## Storing energy

You know that your energy comes from nutrients in the food you eat. Most energy that is not used is stored as fat in the subcutaneous layer of the skin to be used at a later time. Whenever your body requires extra energy, some of the stored energy is returned to your blood and carried to the parts of your body that need it. If a person is overweight, the subcutaneous layer is storing too much energy.

## Gathering information

Your skin is one of your main means of gathering information. Nerve endings in the dermis receive messages of touch, pressure, heat, cold, and pain to send to

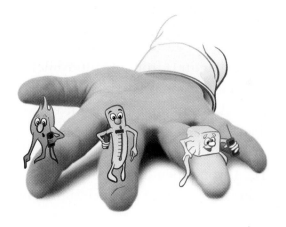

the brain. The nerve endings that are sensitive to pain and extreme heat and cold extend through the dermis to the deepest layer of the epidermis; thus, if this layer of skin is cut, you feel pain. Can you think of other ways your body gathers information to send to your brain?

### Quick Checkup

1. What vitamin is sometimes called the sunshine vitamin?
2. What bone-weakening disease is caused by a lack of vitamin D?

# Guarding against disease

Many diseases and disorders are visible on the skin; therefore, the condition of your skin, hair, and fingernails is often an indication of your overall health.

## Proper nutrients

You know that good nutrition is an important part of good health. Because your skin—including your hair and your nails—is made mostly of *protein,* your body needs sufficient protein in order to grow and repair itself. A lack of protein results in poor resistance to infection and causes wounds to heal slowly.

Adequate *vitamin A* keeps your hair looking shiny and healthy. Dry, rough, or bumpy skin may be a sign of insufficient vitamin A. Fingernails that split or break easily, are extremely thin, or fail to grow indicate a lack of either protein or vitamin A.

Because *vitamin E* helps your body to use vitamin A, it is essential for healthy

skin, too. A lack of *B vitamins* can cause a dry, scaly scalp. *Fats* are also necessary in your diet to keep your skin from becoming dry and flaky.

*Vitamin C* helps your body to resist and fight infection, and it helps wounds to heal properly. A lack of vitamin C can cause slow healing of wounds.

Wounds that heal slowly can also result from insufficient *zinc,* because zinc aids in the growth and repair of injured tissues. Studies show that adequate zinc is especially important during the latter part of the healing process when the layers of the epidermis are healing.

Refer to the chart of nutrients on pages 10 and 11 and name three good sources for each of these nutrients which are necessary for healthy skin. A sufficient amount of these nutrients usually can be obtained by eating a balanced diet of lean meats, milk and milk products, vegetables, fruits, and whole-grain breads and cereals.

## Vigorous exercise

Exercise in the fresh air improves your blood circulation and gives a healthy glow to your cheeks. Because the increased blood flow brings more nutrients to your skin, exercise is of great value as a protection against skin disease. Exercise also helps the skin retain its ability to stretch. That means if you continue to exercise, you will have fewer wrinkles when you get older.

## Sufficient water

Your skin helps prevent your body from becoming dehydrated (dried out). The thin layer of oil on your skin helps prevent too much water from evaporating through your skin. If you do not

## Link Up

Link Up improves running and dodging skills, which make you more agile. To play Link Up, you need several groups of either three or four players. The players in each group stand one behind the other, holding onto the waist of the person in front of him. One player is the *link*. The link tries to link up to one of the groups by putting his hands on the waist of the last player in a group. If he succeeds in linking up with a group, the first player in that group becomes the link.

To prevent the link from hooking onto the last player of a group, each group runs and dodges in order to keep its front player facing the link. After you learn to play the game well, you may want to play with two links. If you have a large number of players, you may add even more links.

drink enough liquids, however, your blood draws water from your body tissues—including your skin—and your body tissues become dry.

When you exercise vigorously in hot weather, your body can lose more than one or two pints of water an hour through perspiration. If you lack sufficient water, your body does not perspire as much as normal, and thus your body cannot keep you cool. Without this cooling process, the body temperature can rise 1.8 degrees Fahrenheit every five to eight minutes.

If your body temperature rises too high, you will feel very tired, and you may have a headache or feel dizzy. Continued lack of water can result in fainting and heat stroke.

### Adequate rest

Fatigue lowers your body's resistance to disease and affects the appearance of your skin. Most skin cells which have been damaged during the day gradually are replaced while you rest. If the body lacks sufficient sleep, the skin loses its healthy appearance. Because your body is still growing, you need from nine to twelve hours of sleep each night.

### Quick Checkup

1. Name four ways to guard against disease.
2. Name some proper nutrients you should get.
3. How many hours of sleep should you get each night?

# Protecting your skin

## Keep your skin moist

Skin that is continually exposed to cold, dry air or to sun, heat, and wind loses moisture. Remember, you need to drink sufficient liquids to replace moisture that is lost. If your skin becomes too dry,

**Healthful Hint**

Do not form the habit of constantly licking your lips, because this can cause a continuous cycle of drying and chapping.

your hands and lips may chap. You can guard against dry, rough, chapped skin by using a lotion or moisturizing cream.

Lotions and creams help protect your skin whenever your body's natural oil (sebum) dries faster than the dermis can produce it.

Because your lips lack the skin's protective outer layer, they are more exposed to the sun, wind, heat, and cold than the rest of your body's covering. Whenever you lick your lips, you remove the oil that protects them, and your lips become dry. The drier your lips feel, the more you want to lick them. A lip gel or ointment can add moisture to dry, cracked lips.

## Use a sunscreen

Fresh air and sunshine are both necessary for good health; however, too much exposure to sunlight can cause a painful sunburn. Your face, ears, and shoulders are especially sensitive to the sun. Besides causing much discomfort, a severe sunburn can become infected if it is not cared for properly.

You are less likely to get a sunburn if you gradually increase the amount of time you spend in the sun. As you tan, melanin that builds up in your skin helps protect you from the sun. Whenever you are in the sun for a long period of time, you need additional protection from a **sunscreen,** *a cream or lotion which screens out harmful ultraviolet rays.* The fairer your skin, the more protection it needs. You should also use a sunscreen when you are outside on overcast days, because the more direct ultraviolet rays penetrate even through the clouds.

Do you know that wet skin burns faster than dry skin? Since wet skin makes you feel cool, you may not know that you are getting burned; however, water on your skin forms tiny beads which act like tiny lenses to focus the ultraviolet rays from the sun onto your skin. The sun's ultraviolet rays are strongest between ten in the morning and three in the afternoon. The sun's harmful ultraviolet rays are even stronger when they are reflected by water or sand. Thus it is better not to swim or play at the beach

between 10 A.M. and 3 P.M. If you are at the beach when the ultraviolet rays are the strongest, be sure you apply a waterproof sunscreen frequently.

Snow and concrete also reflect and intensify the destructive ultraviolet rays of the sun. Remember, you need to beware of overcast days. Because you feel cooler, you may stay out in the sun longer and sunburn easier than on a hot, sunny day.

The most harm caused by overexposure to the sun is **skin cancer**—*the most common form of cancer.* Hundreds of thousands of cases of skin cancer reported in North America every year are the result of overexposure to the ultraviolet rays of the sun. Skin cancer sometimes is caused by constant overexposure to the sun's harmful rays. It can also be caused by just one intense overexposure to the ultraviolet rays of the sun. Thus one severe sunburn can result in skin cancer years later. Remember that the closer you live to the equator and the fairer your skin, the more protection you need from the sun.

## Healthful Habits  *for healthy skin*

Eat a balanced diet.
Drink sufficient water.
Exercise vigorously.
Get adequate rest.
Protect your skin.

## Tickle Your FUNNY Bone

Question:  How did the pig keep from getting sunburned?

Answer:  By covering its skin with oinkment.

## Quick Checkup

1. What do we call a cream or lotion which screens out harmful ultraviolet rays?

2. What is the most harmful disease caused by overexposure to the sun?

# Chapter Checkup

A. Study the diagram of the skin on p. 65.

B. Define each term.
1. antiseptic
2. callus
3. blister
4. dermis
5. epidermis
6. hair follicle
7. melanin
8. pigment
9. sebum
10. subcutaneous
11. sunscreen
12. sweat gland

C. Answer each question.
1. What layer of skin includes hair and nails?
2. What are the four signs of infection?
3. What is the most harmful result of overexposure to the sun?
4. Why is the condition of your skin often an indication of your overall health?

D. List five different functions of the skin.

# Keys to Good Grooming

# chapter 6

You usually feel your best when you are clean and neat. Cleanliness comes from washing with soap and warm water; neatness comes from combing your hair and taking proper care of your clothes. Cleanliness and neatness are both part of good grooming.

## Caring for your skin

Perspiration, oil, and creases in the epidermis all collect dirt on your skin. To keep your skin healthy and to protect your body from disease and infection, you need to bathe frequently. Bathing with warm water and soap removes dried perspiration, dirt, and bacteria that collect on your skin. Bathing helps keep the skin cells in good condition by washing away the dead cells, and it keeps the pores that lead from the oil glands and the sweat glands open.

Perspiration from the sweat glands has no unpleasant odor until the bacteria that are normally present on the skin combine with the liquid. After a shower or a bath, your skin smells good, because you have washed away any unpleasant odors. You may need to use a deodorant to help prevent unpleasant odors. Most deodorants contain chemicals which destroy bacteria on your skin; thus they help control the odor that is produced.

During hot weather you should *bathe every day.* Some days you may need more than one bath. If you do not take a bath every day during cold weather, you need to

**Healthful Hint**

Use a deodorant only after your skin is clean.

at least wash your hands, face, neck, ears, arms, and feet. Any day you do not bathe, it is helpful to rub your whole body with a towel. This brisk rubbing brings more blood to the skin to nourish it and removes dead skin cells.

Because cold weather slows the production of sebum, your skin may feel dry during the winter months. If your skin itches when you have no rash, it probably is dry. Remember, rubbing a lotion or moisturizing cream over your body adds moisture to your skin.

Always use a clean washcloth and carefully wash every part of your skin. Be sure you rinse all the soap off your body; this will also help keep your skin from drying out. After your shower or bath, dry yourself by rubbing with a clean towel. This

not only dries your skin and prevents it from chapping, but it also sends out more oil to keep your skin soft and smooth.

A warm bath or shower before you go to bed gives you a clean, comfortable feeling that helps you to relax and sleep well. Some people prefer to take a cool bath or shower in the morning because it makes them feel refreshed and ready for a new day. If you take a cool bath or shower, use warm water first to wash away the dirt and oil. Warm your body after a cool bath or shower by rubbing briskly with a towel.

## Your face needs special attention

To keep your face clean, you probably need to wash it at least twice a day. Because of the numerous sebaceous glands on your forehead and at the edges of

**Healthful Hint**

Taking a warm shower removes less oil from your skin than soaking in warm water.

your nose, these areas should be cleansed thoroughly to remove any excess oil and the dirt which collect. It is beneficial for your skin to dampen your face before you lather it with soap. You use less soap, and thus it is easier to rinse off all the soap. Thorough rinsing of your facial skin helps your face to feel smooth and moist instead of drawn and tight.

The skin that protects your eyes needs to be washed when you wash your face. Close your eyes; then gently wash around them using a washcloth, soap, and warm water. This will prevent sties from forming on the edges of your eyelids. Be sure to wash the corners of your eyes, too.

Do not forget to wash your ears! They need to be washed every day with a clean washcloth, soap, and warm water. Rinse the soap off your ears and then dry them carefully. If too much wax builds up in your ears, have your doctor remove it.

Do not try to clean out the wax with a cotton swab; the cotton swab might push the wax farther inside.

## Wash your hands frequently

Your hands tell others a great deal about you. If you are clean and neat, your hands and fingernails show this. They also show if you are careless or lazy. Since you use your hands so much for work and play, they need to be washed more often than any other part of your body. Keeping your hands clean helps to prevent the spreading of disease-causing bacteria, which are transmitted very easily to the mouth or eyes. Clean hands also keep you from soiling things you touch.

You should wash your hands with warm, running water and use plenty of soap to remove the dirt and bacteria. Whenever you pick up any trash, wash your hands as soon as possible after throwing it away.

Keep your hands clean!

Wash **before** eating anything.
Wash **before** going anywhere.
Wash **before** holding a baby.
Wash **before** going near a sick person.
Wash **after** being near a sick person.
Wash **after** playing outside.
Wash **after** handling a pet.
Wash **after** going to the bathroom.
Wash **before** going to bed.

When the weather is cold, be sure to dry your hands thoroughly. This helps keep them from becoming rough or chapped. Smooth skin looks and feels better than rough skin, and it is easier to keep clean. Your hands need additional care during the summer, too, if you spend much time swimming. Wet hands are susceptible to dry, cracked skin and infections.

## Quick Checkup

1. When should you apply a deodorant?
2. What part of your body should you wash the most?

# Special care for your fingernails

Dirty fingernails spoil the appearance of an otherwise well-groomed person. If your fingernails are dirty, you should scrub them with soap and a nailbrush when you wash your hands. Because harmful bacteria can collect and multiply under your nails, it is important to keep them as clean as possible.

When your nails are kept trimmed, there is less space for dirt and pathogens to collect. Fingernails should be kept short enough that they will not break easily. Follow the rounded shape of your fingers when you file or trim your fingernails. You should always cut your nails when they are wet. Nails are softer and more pliable when they are wet, and thus they are easier to trim without breaking. It is better to file your nails while they are dry and firm. Soft, wet nails make it difficult to file the edges smooth.

You should never bite your nails, because harmful bacteria from them can enter your body,

and your nails will look ragged and ugly. If you bite your nails often, they will become thick and uneven. Nails that are bitten close to the skin may become sore and also will allow harmful bacteria to enter the body through breaks in the skin.

The **cuticle,** or *hardened skin around a nail,* helps prevent disease-causing bacteria from entering your body. Your cuticles have very little oil in them, and thus a cuticle may crack easily and get rough edges. If these rough edges tear into the sensitive skin, this causes a condition known as a **hangnail.** Hangnails can become quite painful and may even cause an infection by allowing bacteria to enter the bloodstream.

When you wash your hands, the warm water and soap softens your cuticles. While the cuticles are soft, push them back gently with a towel as you dry your hands. This helps to prevent hangnails. If your hands are extremely dry and cracked, you may need to use hand lotion to keep your cuticles moist and soft.

If your fingernails split, break easily, or do not grow, your body may need more protein or more vitamin A. Protein is the nutrient which your body uses for the growth and repair of muscles. How many foods do you remember that are rich in protein? Check your answers on the nutrient chart on pages 10 and 11. Vitamin A is found only in foods obtained from animals, such as eggs, whole milk, liver, fish-liver oils, and butter. Good sources of **carotene** [kăr′ə·tēn′], *a nutrient which your body changes into vitamin A,* include dark green vegetables and deep yellow fruits and vegetables.

## Proper care of your feet

Your feet should be washed daily with soap and warm water. Be sure to dry them thoroughly, especially between your toes. A fungus that lives on warm, moist skin can cause painful infections between the toes. This skin disease, known as **athlete's foot,** causes sores to form between the toes, and the skin on the soles of the feet becomes broken, flaky, red, and itchy. This contagious skin disease is difficult to keep from spreading from person to person; however, the infection often can be prevented by keeping the skin between the toes clean and dry. Keeping your feet dry also helps to prevent smelly feet.

The best time to care for your toenails is after a warm bath when the nails and the cuticles around them are soft. Toenails should be cut straight across instead of rounded, and they should not be trimmed too close to the skin. Proper trimming prevents the nails from cutting into the flesh. If the toenails are trimmed too close, a corner of the nail may grow

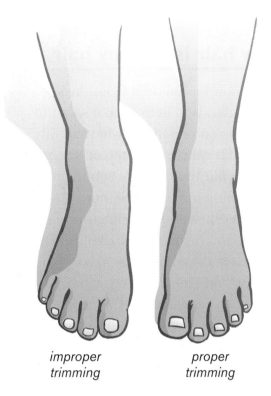

*improper trimming*  *proper trimming*

under the skin, causing an **ingrown toenail.** If the toes are squeezed into tight shoes, an ingrown toenail can become infected. Ingrown toenails can be prevented by cutting your nails properly and by wearing well-fitting shoes.

Tickle Your **FUNNY** Bone

**Question:** If an athlete gets athlete's foot, what does an astronaut get?

**Answer:** Missile toe.

## Shiny hair is healthy hair

Your hair has oil on it from the sebaceous glands to help keep it soft and shiny. Do you remember what this oily substance is called? The oil, or sebum, prevents your hair from becoming too dry and breaking too easily. Sebum, however, also makes dust and dirt cling more easily to your hair. If you do not shampoo often enough, excess sebum may make your hair look and feel oily. The sebum which collects on the scalp mixes with perspiration, bacteria, dead skin cells, and dirt to clog the pores.

Shampooing removes dust and dirt as well as excess oil from your hair and keeps the pores on your scalp open. You normally need to shampoo your hair at least once a week to prevent scalp diseases and unpleasant odors and to keep your hair looking attractive. If you are active outside, perspire heavily, or have an oily scalp, you probably need to shampoo more often.

### Caring for your hair

Always get your hair wet before applying shampoo. Then you will need less shampoo, and your hair will be easier to rinse. One application of shampoo is usually enough. You should not pour the shampoo directly onto your head, because

you will use more shampoo than you need. Pour the shampoo into your hands, rub them together, and then gently massage the shampoo into your hair.

**Healthful Hint**

Excessive use of a blow dryer on a high heat setting can cause scalp dryness and dry, brittle hair.

Rinse your hair thoroughly with warm water until all of the shampoo is removed. If all of the shampoo is not rinsed from your hair, your hair will look oily or dull, and it may feel sticky when it is dry. If you shampoo regularly and always rinse your hair thoroughly, but it still looks oily, you may need to use a different brand of shampoo. Some shampoos have wax in them to make the shampoo thicker. With frequent use, this wax builds up on the hair, causing it to look oily.

Because wet hair can be stretched to almost twice its normal length, it will break easily. Thus you should never brush or comb soaking-wet hair. Either towel dry or blow dry your hair before you comb it.

When combing your hair, never start at your scalp and pull a comb through

**Proper way to comb wet hair**

to remove tangles and snarls. You should first separate any tangles with your fingers. Then, using a wide-toothed comb, begin at the ends of your hair and gently comb down, gradually working up to your scalp. Your hair should be cut or trimmed often enough to keep it looking neat. Hair that is trimmed is easier to brush and comb.

Even if you are taking proper care of your hair but it looks dry and dull and breaks easily, you probably are lacking essential nutrients. Remember—protein and vitamin A help keep your skin, fingernails, and hair looking healthy. How many foods can you name that are rich in vitamin A or carotene?

## Quick Checkup

1. How should fingernails be trimmed?
2. When should nails be trimmed?
3. When should nails be filed?
4. What is another name for the hardened skin around a nail?
5. What is torn skin along a nail which becomes sore called?
6. What are two nutrients your body needs for healthy skin, hair, and nails?
7. What is the nutrient your body changes into vitamin A?

**Tickle Your FUNNY Bone**

**Question:** How does a rabbit stay well groomed?

**Answer:** It uses a hare brush.

## Keeping lice away

Head lice, tiny insects that can infest your hair, suck blood from the scalp, causing it to itch. A female louse normally lives only one month. Each night, she lays about six tiny, white eggs, known as **nits.** Head lice attach their nits to hairs (close to the scalp) with a gummy substance. In six to ten days, the nits hatch, resulting in more lice and then more nits.

Head lice cannot leap or hop from person to person; they usually are spread through direct contact of people's heads. Because head lice can travel quickly from one head to another, however, they spread easily to others at home and at school.

A person who becomes infested with lice should use a specially medicated shampoo to kill the lice and the nits. A second shampooing is usually recommended in seven days.

# Dressing for good health

## Keep your clothes clean

Wearing clean clothes is also part of good personal hygiene. The clothes next to your skin become soiled from perspiration, oil, and bacteria on the epidermis; thus they should be changed daily to protect your body from diseases.

Your mother probably washes your clothes and keeps them mended, but it is your responsibility to help keep them clean and neat. When you get home from school, you should change your clothes before you go outside to work or play. Your outer clothing sometimes can be worn more than one time before it has to be washed or cleaned.

If you can wear your school clothes another day, be sure you neatly hang them in your closet or fold them and put them in your dresser. If you just shove them into a drawer or drop them on the furniture or floor, they will wrinkle. Because you always want to look and feel your best, you must keep your clothes neat. If something needs to be mended, be sure you tell your mother about it. When your clothes are dirty or soiled, put them with the clothes to be washed.

Because your feet perspire, you need to wear clean socks every day. If your socks are not kept clean, your feet will have an unpleasant odor, and you may get athlete's foot, causing your feet to itch or become sore. Wearing clean socks will also help keep the inside of your shoes clean. Do you regularly clean and polish your shoes? Your shoes as well as your clothes will wear longer and look nicer if they are cared for properly.

Before you go to bed, you should change your clothes again. You should not sleep in any of the same clothes that you wore during the day, and your nightgown or pajamas need to be clean and fresh.

## Choose appropriate clothes

You should always wear clothes that are suitable for your age and suitable for what you are doing. Clothes that you wear to church are not appropriate to wear hiking, but they may be appropriate to wear to school. Are clothes that you wear to a music recital or to a party appropriate for horseback riding? The shoes you wear should also be suitable for what you are doing. Some shoes do not give your feet enough support to prevent injuries while you are physically active.

To look well dressed, you do not need new or expensive clothes, but your clothes must be clean and neat. They should fit you well and look becoming on you. Of course, wrinkled or soiled clothes are never becoming. If your clothes are the right size, but they do not look attractive on you, you may need to practice good posture habits. Poor posture can cause your clothes to fit poorly. You should avoid wearing tight, uncomfortable clothes, because they can interfere with the circulation of your blood.

**Healthful Hint**

Wear only clean clothes.

How would you describe a person with poor grooming habits? Would you say he is careless? Lazy? Good personal hygiene is important to your health, because it helps to prevent the spreading of diseases. Good grooming also affects the way you feel and the way others feel about you. When you are clean and neat and your clothes are appropriate for the occasion, you feel happy and full of energy. You know that you look well, and thus you feel more comfortable around others.

## Quick Checkup

1. What insects can infect hair?
2. What are their eggs called?
3. Name some ways head lice are spread.

**Healthful Hint**

If you want others to think well of you, keep yourself clean and neat.

# Cleanliness begins at home

It is easier to be well groomed if you have good hygiene habits at home. Your mother works hard to keep your home clean. Do you help her by cleaning your bedroom? A good motto to help keep your room clean and neat is—*A place for everything and everything in its place.*

## Avoid spreading dust

When you dust your bedroom, it is helpful to use a cloth which has been slightly dampened with water or sprayed with a cleaner. The damp or oiled cloth will pick up the dust and not scatter it. Do you regularly vacuum the floor to pick up dust and dirt? A vacuum cleaner scatters less dust than a broom. When you vacuum, do you use the correct posture for vacuuming? Remember, poor posture can make you tire easily, or it can hurt your back.

## Sparkling is clean

Do you sometimes help clean the kitchen after you eat? The kitchen should

Help clean the kitchen carefully.

Is all of the food put away?

Are the clean dishes put in the cupboard?

Are any crumbs left on the counters or on the table?

Is the stove washed?

Is the sink cleaned?

Does the floor need to be vacuumed or swept?

be one of the cleanest rooms in your house, because bacteria spread easily from hands, clothes, and surroundings to food. The bacteria then infect the body when the food is eaten.

If it is your job to take out the trash, make sure the lid tightly covers the garbage can. Flies, ants, and cockroaches that get into garbage cans spread disease-causing bacteria.

The bathroom, where you usually wash, must also be clean to avoid spreading harmful bacteria. Each time you use the bathroom, you should leave it clean and neat for the next person. Do you cheerfully and willingly do your part to keep your home clean? When you help clean your house, you are helping to keep yourself and your family healthy.

## Sprint and Pass Relay

Relay races improve your speed and agility for many sports. Sprint and Pass Relay will also help improve your passing and catching skills. To play Sprint and Pass Relay, you need a large playing field or gymnasium and a large ball, such as a basketball, a volleyball, or a soccer ball.

On the playing area, mark two parallel lines 15 feet apart. The length of the lines depends on the number of players on each team. Divide into two teams, with half the players along each line. The players line up about five feet apart, facing the opposing team. The players at the ends of each line must keep one foot touching the end of the line.

The players at the head (one end) of each line hold a ball. On the signal to begin, these two players—called the head players—sprint around behind the opposing team to the other end of their own line. After a head player leaves his position on the line, every player on the team moves up one space. As soon as the head player's foot touches the end of his line, he passes the ball to the next player, who quickly passes it to the next player, and so on until it is passed to the new player at the head of the line. Each player in turn sprints around behind the opposing team and passes the ball forward to the head of the line. The team whose head player is back at the head of the line with the ball in his hands first is the winner.

length will vary

15 feet

## Healthful Habits for good grooming

Bathe daily. Wash your hands frequently.

Keep your fingernails clean. Shampoo your hair regularly.

Wear clothes which are clean and neat.

# Chapter Checkup

A. Complete each statement.

1. During hot weather, you should bathe ___?___ .

2. You should trim your nails when they are ___?___ .

3. You should file your nails when they are ___?___ .

4. The hardened skin around a nail is the ___?___ .

5. A torn cuticle which becomes sore is a ___?___ .

6. A skin disease which causes sores between the toes and on the soles of the feet is known as ___?___ .

7. Two nutrients which are necessary for healthy skin, hair, and nails are ___?___ and ___?___ .

8. To look well dressed, your clothes must be ___?___ and ___?___ .

9. Good hygiene helps to prevent the spreading of ___?___ .

10. Cleanliness begins at ___?___ .

B. Answer each question.

1. Which part of your body needs to be washed most often?

2. Which nutrient does your body change into vitamin A?

3. How can ingrown toenails be prevented?

4. Why should you dampen your hair before applying shampoo?

5. Why should you not comb your hair when it is soaking wet?

6. How does keeping the kitchen clean help prevent the spread of diseases?

# A Healthier You

# chapter 7

Your thoughts and feelings affect many functions of your body, and thus they also affect your physical health. A right relationship with others can help you to have happy, healthy thoughts, resulting in a happier, healthier life.

## A new life in Christ

The Bible says that "the life of the flesh is in the blood" (Lev. 17:11). Just as the blood in your body gives you physical life, the shed blood of Jesus Christ can give you spiritual life. When Jesus died on the cross, He died to take your punishment for sin so that you might have everlasting (spiritual) life. After Jesus rose from the dead, He returned to Heaven, where He is living today. Have you trusted Jesus as your Savior from sin? If so, Jesus is preparing a place for you in His heavenly home. Read John 14:2–6 in your Bible. Which verse tells you the only way to get to Heaven?

## A healthy relationship with God

To have good physical health, you need nutritious food, regular exercise, adequate rest, and frequent cleansing. When you become a Christian, these same things are necessary for a healthy spiritual life.

### Daily spiritual food

In order to grow spiritually, you need spiritual food. Jesus said, "I am the *bread of life:* he that cometh to Me shall never hunger; and he that believeth on Me shall never thirst" (John 6:35). You learn more about Jesus by reading God's Word. Just as eating good food every day helps to keep your body healthy, so reading and studying the Bible daily helps you to have good spiritual health. From reading the Bible, you can learn what God is like, why He made you, and what He wants you to do. If you read about doing right, such as being obedient, being truthful, or being kind, God wants you to practice it. If you read about God's care, thank Him for it. If God gives you a promise, claim it.

## Regular spiritual exercise

In order to become a strong, healthy Christian, you need regular spiritual exercise. Do others know from your actions that you are a Christian? Jesus said, "Let your light so shine before men, that they may see your good works, and glorify your Father which is in heaven" (Matt. 5:16). Do the things you say and do always show

that you love God? If you want to control what you say or do, you must control your thoughts. The Bible teaches, "For as he thinketh in his heart, so is he" (Prov. 23:7). Thus, you need to be careful what you read, what you listen to, and what you see, because things that you see or hear every day are stored in your mind.

When you spend time reading and studying the Bible, your mind is filled with thoughts that are true, honest, just, pure, and lovely. It is impossible for you to have these kinds of thoughts from questionable television programs or reading material or the words of unwholesome music, such as rock and rap music. Wrong thoughts can affect your spiritual health, your mental health, and your physical health. Good, wholesome reading—from the Bible and good books and magazines—and listening to good music will help you to have right thoughts so that you can be the kind of Christian God wants you to be.

**Healthful Hint**

The Bible says, "Study to show thyself approved unto God, a workman that needeth not to be ashamed, rightly dividing the word of truth" (2 Tim. 2:15).

One of the best ways to show that you love God is to be obedient. Jesus said, "If ye love Me, keep My commandments" (John 14:15). A good commandment for you to memorize is Col. 3:20. "Children, obey your parents in all things: for this is well pleasing unto the Lord." Do you always obey when you are asked to do something? Do you obey promptly and cheerfully? If you grumble and complain while you complete a task, will others see God's love?

Witnessing for Jesus also strengthens your spiritual life. How often do you tell others that Jesus loves them and that He died for them? When right thoughts are in your mind, it is easier to tell others about Jesus, and it is easier to show your love for Him.

## Adequate spiritual rest

Another requirement for a healthy Christian life is spiritual rest, or a quiet time with God. Do you get so busy going to school, doing homework and chores, and playing that you neglect to spend time with God? Just as a time of rest refreshes your body, so a quiet time with God refreshes deep inside you. "They that wait upon the Lord shall renew their strength; they shall mount up with wings as eagles; they shall run, and not be weary; and they shall walk, and not faint" (Isa. 40:31).

### Quick Checkup

1. What are two ways to have a healthy relationship with God?

2. How do you get daily spiritual food?

3. How do you get regular spiritual exercise?

Since God is everywhere, you can spend time with Him wherever you are. If you are outside, you can learn about Him through His creation. "The heavens declare the

## I Don't Have to Wait

I don't have to wait until I'm grown up
 To be loving and true;
There are many little deeds of kindness
 That each day I can do.

Ev'ry day my body is made stronger
 As I eat, play, and sleep;
And I'll daily grow more like the Savior,
 If His Word I will keep.

I can read my Bible and pray,
 Be a loving helper alway;
I don't have to wait until I'm grown up
 To be what Jesus wants me to be.
 —Harold Deal

glory of God; and the firmament showeth His handiwork" (Psa. 19:1). God is a God of beauty. He is powerful. He is wise. He is good. When was the last time you thanked God for His goodness to you? God wants you to spend time talking to Him. You can thank Him for the fun times, and you can tell Him about the sad times. He is always ready to listen.

Although you can pray at any time, one of the best times to talk to God is when you wake up in the morning. You should thank Him for His care throughout the night, and you can ask Him for His help during the day—especially those times when you know you will need help to do right. Do you listen when God reminds you "Be ye kind one to another" (Eph. 4:32) or "Children, obey your parents in all things" (Col. 3:20)? Ask God to help you obey these commandments.

## Frequent spiritual cleansing

Even though you are a Christian, you will sometimes sin. Whenever you sin, although God still loves you, He is grieved, and your right relationship with God is broken. You no longer feel like spending time with God.

Continuing in sin not only affects your spiritual health, but it can also affect your physical health. If you are not truthful or are unkind, you may feel unhappy or be upset. Allowing wrong thoughts—such as anger, jealousy, bitterness, and self-pity —to remain in your mind also affects how you feel. Such unpleasant feelings interfere with the digestion of your food and prevent you from sleeping well, causing you to become ill.

Every time you sin, you need spiritual cleansing. Do you know how to be cleansed so that a right relationship with God is renewed? "If we confess our sins, He is faithful and just to forgive us our sins, and to cleanse us from all unrighteousness" (1 John 1:9). God wants you *to feel* sorry and *to say* "I'm sorry." First, you need

to tell God that you are sorry for your sin. Then, if you wronged someone else by your sin, you need to apologize to that person. If you are truly sorry, God will forgive you and cleanse you from your sin.

As soon as a right relationship with God is restored, you will again feel like talking to God and singing praises to Him. "I will praise Thee, O Lord, with my whole heart; I will show forth all Thy marvelous works. I will be glad and rejoice in Thee: I will sing praise to Thy name, O Thou most High" (Psa. 9:1–2).

## A good relationship with others

When you care about someone, it shows in what you say and how you act. Are you thoughtful of others? God commands us to "be courteous" (1 Pet. 3:8). **Courtesy** is being polite and loving to others at all times.

### Being thoughtful of others

If you think only about yourself and what you like, you are being selfish—a selfish person is usually an unhappy person. When you think of ways to help other people, you will think less about yourself. Showing kindness by the things you say and the things you do tells others that you care about them. Because you make them happy, you feel happy, too.

Cheerfulness is an important part of courtesy, because it makes others happy.

Question: What did the polite lamb say to its mother?

Answer: Thank ewe.

Question: What do you call a young hippo with bad table manners?

Answer: A hippopotamess.

When you smile at others, you will receive many smiles in return. It is always easy to be cheerful when you are happy and having fun. Are you also cheerful when you are asked to help do something? How pleasant it sounds to hear the reply, "I'll be glad to." Do you say only pleasant things? If what you have to say is not kind or pleasant, you should not say anything at all. No one likes to listen to a grumbler, a complainer, or a whiner.

Sometimes it is not *what* you say that is unpleasant. It sounds unpleasant because of the *way* you say it. Say "I'll help you" in a pleasant way. If you are thinking of others, you will want to help. Now say "I'll help you" in a grumbling or a complaining way. Which way shows that you are thinking of others instead of yourself? Remember that a habit is something you do without thinking about it. If you try each day to be cheerful about what you do and say, cheerfulness will soon become a good habit.

## Caring about your family

You do not live alone; you live with other people. If courtesy is really a part of you, you will be just as courteous to those in your family as you are to others. You will cheerfully do or say whatever you can to help make your home a pleasant place to live. Do you do your chores at home without being told? Are you willing to help your brothers or sisters with their

responsibilities when they need help? Sometimes responsibilities can be more interesting if you make them into a game. Every day when you make your bed, time yourself with a stopwatch or a clock that has a second hand. Try to make your bed well—without wrinkles—in record time.

As you learn to live, to work, and to play together as a family, a special closeness develops among the members of your family. If you have this good relationship with your family, you will want to share with them the exciting things that happened during your day. You will want to share your successes and happy feelings. You also will want to share your troubles and feelings of sorrow. Because your mother and father love you, they care about what you do. They want to comfort you and to give you guidance and direction in your life. When was the last time you told your mother and father "I love you"? Do you "obey your parents in all things" (Col. 3:20) to show them that you care about them?

## Choosing the right friends

The Bible says, "A man that hath friends must show himself friendly" (Prov. 18:24). Who are your friends? Do they enjoy doing many of the same things that you enjoy? It is important for you to have good friends to talk to and to do things with. You can share many good times together. Because you spend more time with your friends as you grow older, it is essential to have the right friends.

You should never be close friends with boys or girls who do things that you or your parents do not approve of. The wrong friends can cause you to have wrong thoughts, which will lead to wrongdoing. Good friends will encourage you

in right relationships at home and in a right relationship with God. When you have a right relationship with God, with your family, and with your friends, you feel good about yourself, and you share your good feelings with those around you.

**Healthful Hint**

Maintain a close relationship with your parents.

## Throw and Catch

*Many active games can help you learn some of the skills you will need for playing sports. Throwing and catching are important skills for softball, baseball, and football.*

To play Throw and Catch, you need a tennis ball or a softball and a playing field with a goal line marked at each end of the field. The goal lines should be from 10 to 15 yards apart, depending on the skill of the players. Any number of players can participate.

Divide into two teams and line up behind the goal lines as pictured in the illustration. The first player on one team throws the ball to the opposing team. The players on the opposing team must stand behind the goal line until the ball is thrown. If the ball crosses the goal line and is caught by any player on the opposing team before it touches the ground, no point is scored. If the ball crosses the goal line but is not caught before it touches the ground, the thrower's team scores one point. If the ball is not thrown hard enough to cross the goal line, any player on the opposing team may run forward to catch it. If it is caught, the catcher's team scores one point.

The teams take turns throwing and catching. The game should move quickly so that the players are kept active. If your teams are very large, you may want to use two balls so that every player has an opportunity to throw the ball. Then, two players on the same team throw a ball when a signal is given. The team with the most points at the end of the playing period is the winner. For variety, you may toss and catch a football using the same rules.

**Healthful Habits** for a healthier you

Practice good posture.
Exercise regularly.
Get adequate rest.
Eat a variety of foods.
Drink sufficient water.

Be clean and neat.
Be thoughtful of others.
Choose good friends.
Be right with God.

# Glossary

## A

**abdomen** (ăb′də·mən), *n.*
the part of the body containing the stomach, the intestines, and other important organs

**abdominal** (ăb·dŏm′ə·nəl), *adj.*
of, in, on, or for the abdomen

**abrasion** (ə·brā′zhən), *n.*
a scraped area of skin

**adenoid** (ăd′n·oid′), *n.*
a growth of tissue at the back of the nasal passage which helps fight infection

**aerobics** (â·rō′bĭks), *n.*
a type of exercise which strengthens the lungs and heart

**agile** (ăj′əl), *adj.*
able to move quickly and easily

**AIDS** (ādz: acquired immune deficiency syndrome), *n.*
a disease (probably caused by a virus) which destroys the body's immune system; it does not commonly affect children

**albino** (ăl·bī′nō), *n.*
a person whose skin has no pigment (coloring matter)

**alveoli** (ăl·vē′ə·lī), *n.*
air sacs in the lungs; *sing.*, **alveolus** (ăl·vē′ə·ləs)

**antiseptic** (ăn′tĭ·sĕp′tĭk), *n.*
a substance which destroys many pathogens (germs)

**athlete's foot** (ăth′lēts fŏŏt), *n.*
a skin disease which causes sores between the toes and on the soles of the feet

## B

**balanced diet** (băl′ənst dī′ĭt), *n.*
a variety of foods containing all the nutrients necessary for good health

**biceps** (bī′sĕps′), *n.*
a muscle at the front of the upper arm

**bicuspid** (bī·kŭs′pĭd), *n.*
a tooth having two points, or cusps, which function to crush food; located next to the cuspids

**blister** (blĭs′tər), *n.*
a raised part of epidermis (the outer layer of skin) which is filled with a watery substance; caused by excessive rubbing or burning

**breathing** (brē′t͟hĭng), *n.*
external respiration; the process by which air enters and leaves the body

**bronchi** (brŏng′kī), *n.*
the two branches at the lower end of the trachea (windpipe); *sing.*, **bronchus** (brŏng′kəs)

**bronchial tube** (brŏng′kē·əl tūb), *n.*
a tube branching from the bronchi

**bronchioles** (brŏng′kē·ōlz), *n.*
the smallest bronchial tubes

## C

**calcium** (kăl′sē·əm), *n.*
a mineral contained in food and needed by the body; helps form strong bones and teeth

**calculus** (kăl′kyə·ləs), *n.*
a hardened buildup of plaque

**calisthenics** (kăl′ĭs·thĕn′ĭks), *n.*
exercises which build muscular strength through repeated movements

**callus** (kăl′əs), *n.*
a thick, hard layer of epidermis (outer layer of skin)

**cancer** (kăn′sər), *n.*
a harmful growth that destroys healthy body parts

**carbon dioxide** (kär′bən dī·ŏk′sīd), *n.*
a waste gas which the body exhales (breathes out)

**cardiac** (kär′dē·ăk′), *adj.*
of, near, or affecting the heart

**carotene** (kăr′ə·tēn), *n.*
a nutrient which the body changes into vitamin A

**carpal** (kär′pəl), *n.*
one of eight wrist bones

**cartilage** (kär′tl·ĭj), *n.*
a tough, solid tissue which forms part of the skeleton

**cementum** (sǐ·měn′təm), *n.*
a thin covering over the root of a tooth which holds the tooth firmly together

**cilia** (sǐl′ē·ə), *n.*
the hairlike structures along the surface of the mucous membrane in the air passageways; *sing.,* **cilium** (sǐl′ē·əm)

**clavicle** (klăv′ǐ·kəl), *n.*
a collarbone

**contract** (kən·trăkt′), *v.*
to tighten, to shorten, or to become smaller

**courtesy** (kûr′tǐ·sē), *n.*
being polite and loving to others

**cramp** (krămp), *n.*
a sudden, painful muscle contraction

**cranium** (krā′nē·əm), *n.*
the bones of the skull that enclose the brain

**crown** (kroun), *n.*
the part of a tooth that can be seen above the gum line

**cusp** (kŭsp), *n.*
a point on the crown of a tooth

**cuspid** (kŭs′pǐd), *n.*
a tooth having one point, or cusp, which functions to tear apart food; located next to the incisors

**cuticle** (kyōō′tǐ·kəl), *n.*
the hardened skin around a nail

### D

**dental caries** (děn′təl kâr′ēz), *n.*
decay of teeth; cavities

**dental hygienist** (děn′təl hī·jē′nǐst), *n.*
a person trained to remove calculus from teeth; a dentist's assistant

**dentin** (děn′tǐn), *n.*
a hard, bonelike tissue which forms and shapes a tooth

**dermis** (dûr′mǐs), *n.*
the layer of skin beneath the epidermis

**diaphragm** (dī′ə·frăm), *n.*
a flat sheet of muscle which separates the chest cavity from the abdominal cavity; the movable floor of the rib cage that causes the lungs to expand

### E

**enamel** (ǐ·năm′əl), *n.*
the substance which covers the crown of a tooth; the hardest substance in the body

**endurance** (ěn·dōōr′əns), *n.*
the ability to keep on

**epidermis** (ěp′ǐ·dûr′mǐs), *n.*
the outer layer of skin

**epiglottis** (ěp′ǐ·glŏt′ǐs), *n.*
a tiny flap of cartilage that covers the trachea (windpipe) during swallowing

**exhale** (ěks·hāl′), *v.*
to breathe out

**external respiration** (ǐk·stûr′nəl rěs′pə·rā′shən), *n.*
the process by which air enters and leaves the body; breathing

### F

**facial** (fā′shəl), *adj.*
of or for the face

**femur** (fē′mər), *n.*
the thighbone, or bone in the upper leg

**fibula** (fǐb′yə·lə), *n.*
the calf bone of the lower leg

**floss** (flôs), *n.*
a thin, strong thread for removing food particles from between the teeth; *v.* to clean the teeth with dental floss

**fluoride** (flōōr′īd), *n.*
a mineral which strengthens the enamel on a tooth

**frontalis** (frŏn·tăl′ǐs), *n.*
a facial muscle that raises the eyebrows

### H

**habit** (hăb′ǐt), *n.*
something a person does without thinking about it

**hair follicle** (hâr fŏl′ǐ·kəl), *n.*
a little sac in the dermis (the middle layer of skin) in which the root of a hair grows

**halitosis** (hăl′ǐ·tō′sǐs), *n.*
bad smelling breath

**hamstrings** (hăm′strǐngs′), *n.*
three muscles in the back of the upper leg

**hangnail** (hăng′nāl′), *n.*
torn skin along the side or bottom of a fingernail or a toenail

**humerus** (hyoo′mər·əs), *n.*
the bone of the upper arm

**hygiene** (hī′jēn′), *n.*
cleanliness

## I

**immovable** (ĭm·moo′və·bəl), *adj.*
cannot be moved

**incisor** (ĭn·sī′zər), *n.*
a front tooth which functions to bite and cut food

**infection** (ĭn·fĕk′shən), *n.*
result of being infected by pathogens

**inflame** (ĭn·flām′), *v.*
to become red and swollen

**ingrown toenail** (ĭn′grōn′ tō′nāl′), *n.*
a corner of the toenail that grows under the skin

**inhale** (ĭn·hāl′), *v.*
to breathe in

**involuntary muscle** (ĭn·vŏl′ən·tĕr′ē mŭs′əl), *n.*
a muscle which a person cannot consciously control

**isometrics** (ī′sə·mĕt′rĭks), *n.*
a type of exercise in which the muscles contract without moving the body

## J

**joint** (joint), *n.*
a place where bones join

## L

**larynx** (lăr′ĭngks), *n.*
the voice box

**ligament** (lĭg′ə·mənt), *n.*
a band of tough fibers which holds bones together

**limber** (lĭm′bər), *adj.*
able to bend easily

**louse** (lous), *n.*
a wingless insect which lives on a person's skin; a head louse infests the hair and sucks blood from the scalp, causing it to itch

**lung** (lŭng), *n.*
one of two large organs in which the exchange of oxygen and carbon dioxide occurs

**lung cancer** (lŭng kăn′sər), *n.*
a cancer that is most often associated with smoking cigarettes

## M

**malocclusion** (măl′ə·kloo′zhən), *n.*
the improper fitting together of the upper and lower teeth

**masseter** (mă·sē′tər), *n.*
a muscle which extends from the cheekbone to the chin

**melanin** (mĕl′ə·nĭn), *n.*
a dark-colored pigment which gives the skin a brownish color

**metabolism** (mĭ·tăb′ə·lĭz′əm), *n.*
the process by which the body produces and uses energy from food

**metacarpal** (mĕt′ə·kär′pəl), *n.*
a bone of the hand

**metatarsal** (mĕt′ə·tär′səl), *n.*
a bone of the foot

**microorganism** (mī′krō·ôr′gə·nĭz′əm), *n.*
a tiny, living thing that can be seen only through a microscope; also called **microbe** (mī′krōb′)

**molar** (mō′lər), *n.*
a tooth located in the back portion of the mouth which functions to grind food

**motor nerve** (mō′tər nûrv), *n.*
a nerve which carries messages from the brain and spinal cord to the muscles

**mucous membrane** (myoo′kəs mĕm′brān′), *n.*
the moist lining inside the openings to the body

**mucus** (myoo′kəs), *n.*
a sticky fluid produced by the mucous membrane

**muscle strain** (mŭs′əl strān), *n.*
any damage to a muscle that causes pain

**muscle tone** (mŭs′əl tōn), *n.*
the constant, slight contraction of muscle fibers in a skeletal muscle

# N

**nasal** (nā′zəl), *adj.*
of the nose

**nicotine** (nĭk′ə·tēn′), *n.*
a poisonous substance contained in tobacco

**nit** (nĭt), *n.*
the egg of a louse

# O

**orthodontist** (ôr′thə·dŏn′tĭst), *n.*
a dentist who specializes in treating malocclusion (the improper fitting together of the upper and lower teeth)

**oxygen** (ŏk′sĭ·jən), *n.*
a gas contained in the air which the body inhales (breathes in)

# P

**paralysis** (pə·răl′ĭ·sĭs), *n.*
loss of ability to move

**patella** (pə·tĕl′ə), *n.*
the kneecap

**pathogen** (păth′ə·jən), *n.*
a disease-causing microorganism (a tiny, living thing that can be seen only through a microscope)

**periodontal** (pĕr′ē·ə·dŏn′təl), *adj.*
affecting the gums

**periodontal disease** (pĕr′ē·ə·dŏn′təl dĭ·zēz′), *n.*
a disease affecting the tissues and bones that support the teeth; gum disease

**periodontal membrane** (pĕr′ē·ə·dŏn′təl mĕm′brān′), *n.*
the layer of tissue between the cementum and the jawbone which connects the root of a tooth to the jawbone

**phalanges** (fə·lăn′jēz), *n.*
the finger or toe bones; *sing.,* **phalanx** (fā′lăngks′)

**pharynx** (făr′ĭngks), *n.*
the throat

**pigment** (pĭg′mənt), *n.*
coloring matter

**plaque** (plăk), *n.*
a sticky, colorless film of harmful bacteria which is constantly forming on and between the teeth

**posture** (pŏs′chər), *n.*
the way the body is held while sitting, standing, or moving about

**pulp** (pŭlp), *n.*
the inner part of a tooth, containing nerves and blood vessels

# Q

**quadriceps** (kwŏd′rĭ·sĕps′), *n.*
the muscle in the front of the upper leg

# R

**rickets** (rĭk′ĭts), *n.*
a disease caused by a lack of vitamin D, resulting in weak bones and deformities

**root** (ro͞ot), *n.*
the part of a tooth which anchors the tooth in the jawbone

# S

**saliva** (sə·lī′və), *n.*
a digestive juice in the mouth

**scapula** (skăp′yə·lə), *n.*
a shoulder blade

**sebaceous gland** (sĭ·bā′shəs glănd), *n.*
a gland located in the dermis (the middle layer of skin) which produces sebum (an oily substance)

**sebum** (sē′bəm), *n.*
an oily substance produced by the oil glands in the skin

**sinus** (sī′nəs), *n.*
a cavity (hollow place) in the thick bones of the face

**sinusitis** (sī′nə·sī′tĭs), *n.*
an infection of the sinuses

**skeleton** (skĕl′ĭ·tn), *n.*
the body's framework

**skin cancer** (skĭn kăn′sər), *n.*
a cancer caused by overexposure to harmful ultraviolet rays; the most common form of cancer

**skull** (skŭl), *n.*
the bones of the head

**spinal column** (spī′nəl kŏl′əm), *n.*
the backbone

**sprint** (sprĭnt), *v.*
to run at full speed for a short distance;
*n.* a short, fast run

**sterile** (stĕr′əl), *adj.*
free from pathogens (germs)

**sternum** (stûr′nəm), *n.*
the breastbone

**strain** (strān), *v.*
to injure or weaken by force;
*n.* an injury to a muscle caused by overwork

**subcutaneous** (sŭb′kyoo̅·tā′nē·əs), *adj.*
the fatty layer of skin that stores energy

**sunscreen** (sŭn′skrēn′), *n.*
a cream or lotion which absorbs harmful ultraviolet rays of the sun

**sunshine vitamin** (sŭn′shīn′ vī′tə·mĭn), *n.*
vitamin D; manufactured in the skin with the
aid of sunlight

**sweat gland** (swĕt glănd), *n.*
a gland located in the dermis (the middle
layer of skin) which helps to control the body
temperature and helps to remove excess body
wastes

**synovial fluid** (sĭ·nō′vē·əl floo̅′ĭd), *n.*
the fluid produced in a joint to lubricate
the joint

# T

**tarsal** (tär′səl), *n.*
one of seven ankle bones

**tendon** (tĕn′dən), *n.*
a band of tough fibers which attaches muscle
to bone

**tibia** (tĭb′ē·ə), *n.*
the shinbone of the lower leg

**tonsil** (tŏn′səl), *n.*
a growth of tissue at the back of the throat
which helps fight infection

**trachea** (trā′kē·ə), *n.*
the windpipe

**translucent** (trăns·loo̅′sənt), *adj.*
allows light to pass through but cannot be seen
through clearly

**trapezius** (trə·pē′zē·əs), *n.*
a large skeletal muscle which moves the
scapula (shoulder blade)

**triceps** (trī′sĕps′), *n.*
a muscle at the back of the upper arm

# U

**ultraviolet rays** (ŭl′trə·vī′ə·lĭt rāz), *n.*
harmful, invisible rays of the sun

# V

**vertebra** (vûr′tə·brə), *n.*
one bone of the spinal column; *pl.*, **vertebrae**
(vûr′tə·brā)

**vitamin D** (vī′tə·mĭn dē), *n.*
the "sunshine vitamin"; helps the body to
absorb calcium

**voluntary muscle** (vŏl′ən·tĕr′ē mŭs′əl), *n.*
a muscle which a person is able to consciously
control

# Index

Page numbers for illustrations are printed in *italic type*.

# Credits

Credits are listed from left to right, top to bottom on a page. If all on a page are from the same source, the credit is given only once. All other photos not mentioned are property of the publisher. CC—courtesy Corel Corporation; CB—courtesy Corbis Corporation.

Front Cover—Rubberball (boy/girl), CC (fruit); back cover—BananaStock (girl), Digital Vision (vegetables), CC (tennis equipment); title page—Rubberball; iii—CC; iv, v—CB; 2—Adobe; 3—CC; 4—CB; 8—CB; 15—CB; 17—CB, SuperStock, Inc./SuperStock; 18—Richard Hutchings/Photo Researchers, Inc., CC; 22—CC; 25—L. V. Bergman/The Bergman Collection; 26—Lawrence Migdale/Photo Researchers, Inc., Tom Rosenthal/SuperStock, Jerry Wachter/Photo Researchers, Inc.; 31—Tom Rosenthal/SuperStock; 34—SuperStock, Inc./SuperStock; 35—CC; 37—Ken Lax/SS/ Photo Researchers, Inc.; 38—Ken Cavanagh/Photo Researchers, Inc.; 41—Arthur Glauberman/SS/Photo Researchers, Inc.; 42—Ralph Reinhold/Earth Scenes; 43—Tim Davis/Photo Researchers, Inc., Richard Heinzen/SuperStock; 45—CC; 51—Ken Cavanagh/Photo Researchers, Inc.; 56—Photri; 60—Tom Rosenthal/ SuperStock, Richard Heinzen/SuperStock; 61—CC, CB; 68—Photri; 69—SuperStock, Inc./SuperStock, SuperStock, Inc./SuperStock, CB; 70—Woody Woodworth/ SuperStock, Dr. P. Marazzi/SPL/Photo Researchers, Inc.; 71—SuperStock; 72—CB; 73—CB; 78—Beerman Collection/SuperStock; 80—Photri; 82—Lawrence Migdale/Photo Researchers, Inc.; 83—Aaron Haupt/ Photo Researchers, Inc.; 94—Jeff Isaac Greenberg/ Photo Researchers, Inc.; 97—CB, Bets Anderson/Photri; 98—Adobe; 99—Blair Seitz/Photo Researchers, Inc.; 100—CB.